AMERICAN LABOR

FROM CONSPIRACY
TO
COLLECTIVE BARGAINING

WOMEN IN INDUSTRY

Louis D. Brandeis and Josephine Goldmark

With an introduction by Leon Stein & Philip Taft

ARNO & THE NEW YORK TIMES
NEW YORK   1969

INTRODUCTION

Curt Muller operated a laundry in Portland. He thought he had every right to reach an agreement with his laundresses as to how many hours they would work each day. He therefore violated a law of the State of Oregon that no female should be employed at her work more than ten hours in a single day. For this violation he was arrested, brought to trial, and found guilty.

The case took on more than local interest when it became clear that Muller was prepared to carry it to the Supreme Court. The Court had already dealt with state laws aimed at limiting the workday. In 1898 it had upheld, in *Holden v. Hardy,* an eighthour day for miners, citing the hazards of that occupation. But in 1905 in the Bakeshop case, *Lochner v. New York,* the Court found that limiting bakers' working hours to ten a day or sixty a week was an unfair and unreasonable ground for interfering with the right of free contract.

Once again, resting on the due process clause of the Fourteenth Amendment, the Court preserved bad conditions. It was not moved by the plight of mill workers and factory workers who, without standard rates, piece or time, found that their workday grew longer and longer while their pay remained constant, or even shrank.

As the Muller case headed for the Supreme Court, the National Consumer's League undertook to defend the state law. Its chief officer, Florence Kelley, sought the aid of the famous New York lawyer Joseph H. Choate, who quickly showed his sympathies by retorting to Kelley, "Big, strong Irish laundry women? Why shouldn't they work longer?"

Louis D. Brandeis, who would become a justice of the Supreme Court, volunteered as counsel for the League. Brandeis understood that the Court had decided these limitation cases on the basis of precedents, general knowledge and common understanding, howsoever the Court understood these. Thus the doctrine of laissez-faire had been able to survive previous legislative onslaughts.

To break through this defense Brandeis took a bold, innovative step. He set out to prove to the justices that there was indeed need for limiting the length of the workday on the basis of general knowledge and common understanding if these were expanded to include more than what the lawyers knew. Working with his sister-in-law, Josephine Goldmark, he mustered a small army of researchers who then combed the Columbia University Library, the New York Public Library and the Library of Congress.

Brandeis prepared a brief that had two pages of law and more than one hundred pages of facts. Added to the facts of law were the facts of life—life of women in the twentieth century industrial regime—was depicted by physicians, sociologists, criminologists, and experts in housing and hygiene. Also added were selections from European and American reports by factory inspectors and industrial commissions.

Their opinions were unanimous, some holding that even the ten-hour day was too long for women. But as Brandeis argued his case orally on January 15, 1908, the reaction of the justices, veterans of the earlier cases, was uncertain. Then, speaking for the Court, Justice Brewer took the unusual step of mentioning Brandeis by name and complimenting him on the copiousness of his material. Yes, the Court would again take cognizance of general knowledge but this time as that knowledge had been expanded by Brandeis. He had scored over laissez-faire.

In the next eight years, forty-one states enacted new or improved hour laws for working women.

Leon Stein and Philip Taft

WOMEN IN INDUSTRY

WOMEN IN INDUSTRY

DECISION OF THE UNITED STATES SUPREME
COURT IN CURT MULLER *VS.* STATE
OF OREGON

UPHOLDING THE CONSTITUTIONALITY OF THE OREGON
TEN HOUR LAW FOR WOMEN

AND

BRIEF FOR THE STATE OF OREGON

BY

LOUIS D. BRANDEIS

Assisted by JOSEPHINE GOLDMARK
Publication Secretary National Consumers' League

REPRINTED FOR
THE NATIONAL CONSUMERS' LEAGUE
105 East 22d Street, New York City

TABLE OF CONTENTS

Supreme Court of the United States

OCTOBER TERM, 1907

CURT MULLER, Plaintiff in Error,

v.

THE STATE OF OREGON

BRIEF FOR DEFENDANT IN ERROR

This case presents the single question whether the Statute of Oregon, approved Feb. 19, 1903, which provides that " no female [shall] be employed in any mechanical establishment or factory or laundry " " more than ten hours during any one day," is unconstitutional and void as violating the Fourteenth Amendment of the Federal Constitution.

The decision in this case will, in effect, determine the constitutionality of nearly all the statutes in force in the United States, limiting the hours of labor of adult women, — namely:

Massachusetts

First enacted in 1874 (chap. 221), now embodied in Revised Laws, chap. 106, sec. 24, as amended by Stat. 1902, chap. 435, as follows:

No woman shall be employed in laboring in a manufacturing or mechanical establishment more than ten hours in any one day, except as hereinafter provided in this section, unless a different apportionment in hours of labor is made for the sole purpose of making a shorter day's work for one day of the week; and in no case shall the hours of labor exceed fifty-eight in a week. . . . (Held constitutional in Comm. *v.* Hamilton Mfg. Co., 120 Mass. 383.)

RHODE ISLAND

First enacted in 1885 (chap. 519, sec. 1), now embodied in Stat. 1896, chap. 198, sec. 22 (as amended by Stat. 1902, chap. 994), as follows:

. . . No woman shall be employed in laboring in any manufacturing or mechanical establishment more than fifty-eight hours in any one week; and in no case shall the hours of labor exceed ten hours in any one day, excepting when it is necessary to make repairs or to prevent the interruption of the ordinary running of the machinery, or when a different apportionment of the hours of labor is made for the sole purpose of making a shorter day's work for one day of the week.

LOUISIANA

First enacted in 1886 (Act No. 43), and amended by Acts of 1902 (No. 49); now embodied in Revised Laws (1904, p. 989, sec. 4):

. . . No woman shall be employed in any factory, warehouse, workshop, telephone or telegraph office, clothing, dressmaking, or millinery establishment, or in any place where the manufacture of any kind of goods is carried on, or where any goods are prepared for manufacture, for a longer period than an average of ten hours in any day, or sixty hours in any week, and at least one hour shall be allowed in the labor period of each day for dinner.

CONNECTICUT

First enacted in 1887 (chap. 62, sec. 1), now embodied in General Statutes, Revision 1902, sec. 4691, as follows:

. . . No woman shall be employed in laboring in any manufacturing, mechanical, or mercantile establishment more than ten hours in any day, except when it is necessary to make repairs to prevent the interruption of the ordinary running of the machinery, or where a different apportionment of the hours of labor is made

for the sole purpose of making a shorter day's work for one day
of the week. . . . In no case shall the hours of labor exceed sixty
in a week.

MAINE

First enacted in 1887 (chap. 139, sec. 1), now re-enacted
in Revised Statutes, 1903, chap. 40, sec. 48, as follows:

. . . No woman shall be employed in laboring in any manufacturing or mechanical establishment in the State more than ten
hours in any one day, except when it is necessary to make repairs
to prevent the interruption of the ordinary running of the machinery, or when a different apportionment of the hours of labor
is made for the sole purpose of making a shorter day's work for
one day of the week; and in no case shall the hours of labor exceed
sixty in a week.

There is a further provision that any woman " may
lawfully contract for such labor or any number of hours
in excess of ten hours a day, not exceeding six hours in
any one week or sixty hours in any one year, receiving
additional compensation therefor."

NEW HAMPSHIRE

First enacted in 1887 (chap. 25, sec. 1), now re-enacted
by Stat. 1907, chap. 94, as follows:

No woman . . . shall be employed in a manufacturing or mechanical establishment for more than nine hours and forty minutes
in one day except in the following cases: I. To make a shorter
day's work for one day in the week. II. To make up time lost on
some day in the same week in consequence of the stopping of
machinery upon which such person was dependent for employment.
III. When it is necessary to make repairs to prevent interruption
of the ordinary running of the machinery. In no case shall the
hours of labor exceed fifty-eight in one week.

MARYLAND

First enacted in 1888 (chap. 455), now embodied in
Public General Laws, Code of 1903, art. 100, sec. 1:

No corporation or manufacturing company engaged in manufacturing either cotton or woollen yarns, fabrics or domestics of

any kind, incorporated under the laws of this State, and no officer, agent or servant of such named corporation, . . . and no agent or servant of such firm or person shall require, permit, or suffer its, his, or their employees in its, his, or their service, or under his, its, or their control, to work for more than ten hours during each or any day of twenty-four hours for one full day's work, and shall make no contract or agreement with such employees or any of them providing that they or he shall work for more than ten hours for one day's work during each or any day of twenty-four hours, and said ten hours shall constitute one full day's work.

Section 2 makes it possible for male employees to work longer either to make repairs, or by express agreement.

VIRGINIA

First enacted in 1890 (chap. 193, sec. 1), now embodied in Virginia Code (1904), chap. 178 a, sec. 3657 b, as follows:

No female shall work as an operative in any factory or manufacturing establishment in this State more than ten hours in any one day of twenty-four hours. All contracts made or to be made for the employment of any female . . . as an operative in any factory or manufacturing establishment to work more than ten hours in any one day of twenty-four hours shall be void.

PENNSYLVANIA

First enacted in 1897 (No. 26), and re-enacted in Laws of 1905, No. 226, as follows:

Section 1. That the term " establishment," where used for the purpose of this act, shall mean any place within this Commonwealth other than where domestic, coal-mining, or farm labor is employed; where men, women, or children are engaged, and paid a salary or wages, by any person, firm, or corporation, and where such men, women, or children are employees, in the general acceptance of the term.

Section 3. . . . No female shall be employed in any establishment for a longer period than sixty hours in any one week, nor for a longer period than twelve hours in any one day.

(Certain exceptions covering Saturday and Christmas.)

(Held constitutional in Comm. *v.* Beatty, 15 Pa. Superior Ct. 5.)

New York

First enacted in 1899 (chap. 192, sec. 77), now embodied in Stat. 1907, chap. 507, sec. 77, sub-division 3:

. . . No woman shall be employed or permitted to work in any factory in this State . . . more than six days or sixty hours in any one week; nor for more than ten hours in one day. . . .

A female sixteen years of age or upwards . . . may be employed in a factory more than ten hours a day; (a) regularly in not to exceed five days a week in order to make a short day or a holiday on one of the six working days of the week; (b) irregularly in not to exceed three days a week; provided that no such person shall be required or permitted to work more than twelve hours in any one day or more than sixty hours in any one week, etc.

Nebraska

First enacted in 1899 (chap. 107), now embodied in Compiled Statutes (1905, sec. 7955 a):

No female shall be employed in any manufacturing, mechanical, or mercantile establishment, hotel, or restaurant in this State more than sixty hours during any one week, and ten hours shall constitute a day's labor. The hours of each day may be so arranged as to permit the employment of such female at any time from six o'clock A. M. to ten o'clock P. M.; but in no case shall such employment exceed ten hours in any one day.

(Held constitutional in Wenham v. State, 65 Neb. 400.)

Washington

Enacted in 1901, Stat. 1901, chap. 68, sec. 1, as follows:

No female shall be employed in any mechanical or mercantile establishment, laundry, hotel, or restaurant in this State more than ten hours during any day.

The hours of work may be so arranged as to permit the employment of females at any time so that they shall not work more than ten hours during the twenty-four.

(Held constitutional in State v. Buchanan, 29 Wash. 603.)

The acts in the following States raise somewhat similar questions:

WISCONSIN

First enacted in 1867 (chap. 83, sec. 1), and amended by Stat. 1883, chap. 135, now embodied in Wisconsin Statutes, Code of 1898, sec. 1728, as follows:

> In all manufactories, workshops, or other places used for mechanical or manufacturing purposes the time of labor . . . of women employed therein shall not exceed eight hours in one day; and any employer, stockholder, director, officer, overseer, clerk, or foreman who shall compel any woman . . . to labor exceeding eight hours in any one day, . . . shall be punished by fine not less than five nor more than fifty dollars for each such offence.

NORTH DAKOTA

First enacted in 1877 (Penal Code, sec. 739), now embodied in Revised Code, 1905, sec. 9440, as follows:

> Every owner, stockholder, overseer, employer, clerk, or foreman of any manufactory, workshop, or other place used for mechanical or manufacturing purposes, who, having control, shall compel any woman . . . to labor in any day exceeding ten hours, shall be deemed guilty of a misdemeanor, and upon conviction shall be punished by a fine not exceeding one hundred and not less than ten dollars.

SOUTH DAKOTA

First enacted in 1877 (Penal Code, sec. 739), now embodied in Revised Code, 1903 (Penal Code, sec. 764), as follows:

> Every owner, stockholder, overseer, employer, clerk, or foreman of any manufactory, workshop or other place used for mechanical or manufacturing purposes, who, having control, shall compel any woman . . . to labor in any day exceeding ten hours, shall be deemed guilty of a misdemeanor, and upon conviction, shall be punished by a fine not exceeding one hundred and not less than ten dollars.

OKLAHOMA

First enacted in 1890 (Stat. 1890, chap. 25, article 58, sec. 10), now embodied in Revised Statutes, 1903, chap. 25, article 58, sec. 729, as follows:

Every owner, stockholder, overseer, employer, clerk, or foreman of any manufactory, workshop, or other place used for mechanical or manufacturing purposes, who, having control, shall compel any woman or any child under eighteen years of age, or permit any child under fourteen years of age, to labor in any day exceeding ten hours, shall be deemed guilty of a misdemeanor, and upon conviction shall be punished by fine not exceeding one hundred and not less than ten dollars.

NEW JERSEY *

First enacted in 1892 (chap. 92), now embodied in General Statutes, page 2350, secs. 66 and 67, as follows:

Section 66. . . . fifty-five hours shall constitute a week's work in any factory, workshop, or establishment where the manufacture of any goods whatever is carried on; and the periods of employment shall be from seven o'clock in the forenoon until twelve o'clock noon, and from one o'clock in the afternoon until six o'clock in the evening of every working day except Saturday, upon which last named day the period of employment shall be from seven o'clock in the forenoon until twelve o'clock noon.

Section 67. . . . no woman shall be employed in any factory, workshop, or manufacturing establishment except during the periods of employment hereinbefore mentioned: Provided, That the provisions in this act in relation to the hours of employment shall not apply to or affect any person engaged in preserving perishable goods in fruit-canning establishments or in any factory engaged in the manufacture of glass.

* It has been suggested that this provision has been repealed by a general repealing act of 1904, chap. 83.

COLORADO

Enacted in 1903, Acts of 1903, chap. 138, sec. 3:

No woman . . . shall be required to work or labor for a greater number than eight hours in the twenty-four hour day, in any mill, factory, manufacturing establishment, shop, or store for any person, agent, firm, company, copartnership, or corporation, where such labor, work, or occupation by its nature, requires the woman to stand or be upon her feet, in order to satisfactorily perform her labors, work, or duty in such occupation and employment.

SOUTH CAROLINA

Approved February 19, 1907 (Acts of 1907, No. 223), as follows:

Section 1. Ten hours a day or sixty hours a week shall constitute the hours for working for all operatives and employees in cotton and woollen manufacturing establishments engaged in the manufacture of yarns, cloth, hosiery, and other products for merchandise, except mechanics, engineers, firemen, watchmen, teamsters, yard employees, and clerical force. All contracts for longer hours of work other than herein provided in said manufacturing establishments shall be and the same are hereby null and void; and any person entering into or enforcing such contracts shall be deemed guilty of a misdemeanor in each and every instance, and on conviction in a court of competent jurisdiction shall be fined a sum of money not less than twenty-five or more than one hundred dollars, or imprisonment not exceeding thirty days, provided that nothing herein contained shall be construed as forbidding or preventing any such manufacturing company from making up lost time to the extent of sixty hours per annum, where such lost time has been caused by accident or other unavoidable cause.

ARGUMENT

The legal rules applicable to this case are few and are well established, namely:

First: The right to purchase or to sell labor is a part of the " liberty " protected by the Fourteenth Amendment of the Federal Constitution.

> *Lochner* v. *New York*, 198 U. S. 45, 53.

Second: This right to " liberty " is, however, subject to such reasonable restraint of action as the State may impose in the exercise of the police power for the protection of health, safety, morals, and the general welfare.

> *Lochner* v. *New York*, 198 U. S. 45, 53, 67.

Third: The mere assertion that a statute restricting " liberty " relates, though in a remote degree, to the public health, safety, or welfare does not render it valid. The act must have a " real or substantial relation to the protection of the public health and the public safety."

> *Jacobson* v. *Mass*, 197 U. S. 11, 31.

It must have " a more direct relation, as a means to an end, and the end itself must be appropriate and legitimate."

> *Lochner* v. *New York*, 198 U. S. 45, 56, 57, 61.

Fourth: Such a law will not be sustained if the Court can see that it has no real or substantial relation to public health, safety, or welfare, or that it is " an unreasonable, unnecessary and arbitrary interference with the right of the individual to his personal liberty or to enter into those contracts in relation to labor which may seem to him appropriate or necessary for the support of himself and his family."

But " If the end which the Legislature seeks to accomplish be one to which its power extends, and if the means employed to that end, although not the wisest or best, are yet not plainly and palpably unauthorized by law, then the

Court cannot interfere. In other words, when the validity of a statute is questioned, the burden of proof, so to speak, is upon those " who assail it.

Lochner v. New York, 198 U. S. 45–68.

Fifth: The validity of the Oregon statute must therefore be sustained unless the Court can find that there is no " fair ground, reasonable in and of itself, to say that there is material danger to the public health (or safety), or to the health (or safety) of the employees (or to the general welfare), if the hours of labor are not curtailed."

Lochner v. New York, 198 U. S. 45, 61.

The Oregon statute was obviously enacted for the purpose of protecting the public health, safety, and welfare. Indeed it declares:

" Section 5. Inasmuch as the female employees in the various establishments are not protected from overwork, an emergency is hereby declared to exist, and this act shall be in full force and effect from and after its approval by the Governor."

The facts of common knowledge of which the Court may take judicial notice —

See *Holden* v. *Hardy*, 169 U. S. 366.
   Jacobson v. *Mass*, 197 U. S. 11.
   Lochner v. *New York*, 198 U. S. 481.

establish, we submit, conclusively, that there is reasonable ground for holding that to permit women in Oregon to work in a " mechanical establishment, or factory, or laundry " more than ten hours in one day is dangerous to the public health, safety, morals, or welfare.

These facts of common knowledge will be considered under the following heads:

Part I. Legislation (foreign and American) restricting the hours of labor for women.

Part II. The world's experience upon which the legislation limiting the hours of labor for women is based.

PART FIRST

LEGISLATION RESTRICTING THE HOURS OF LABOR
FOR WOMEN

I. THE FOREIGN LEGISLATION

The leading countries in Europe in which women are
largely employed in factory or similar work have found
it necessary to take action for the protection of their
health and safety and the public welfare, and have enacted
laws limiting the hours of labor for adult women.

About two generations have elapsed since the enactment of the first law. In no country in which the legal
limitation upon the hours of labor of adult women was
introduced has the law been repealed. Practically without exception every amendment of the law has been in
the line of strengthening the law or further reducing the
working time.

(a) GREAT BRITAIN

First law enacted in 1844. The British law of 1844 was
the first statute in any country limiting the hours of labor
for adult women. It simply extended to women the provisions of the Act of 1833, which had restricted the work of
children in textile mills to twelve hours per day. In 1847
the legal working time for women as well as children in
textile mills was reduced to ten hours per day. By further
legislation in 1867, 1878, 1891, and 1901 further restrictions were introduced. The law, subject to certain exceptions allowing overtime, is in substance as follows (Law
of 1901, 1 Edw. VII. ch. 22):

Hours.

Textile Factories. (Sec. 24.)

The period of employment, except on Saturday, shall either begin at 6 A. M. and end at 6 P. M., or begin at 7 A. M. and end at 7 P. M.

There shall be allowed for meals during said period of employment on every day except Saturday not less than two hours, of which one hour at the least shall be before 3 P. M.

Special regulations for a shorter day on Saturdays.

Non-textile Factories and Workshops. (Sec. 26.)

The period of employment, except on Saturdays, shall either begin at 6 A. M. and end at 6 P. M., or begin at 7 A. M. and end at 7 P. M., or begin at 8 A. M. and end at 8 P. M.

There shall be allowed for meals during the said period of employment on every day except Saturday not less than one and one-half hours, of which one hour at the least shall be before 3 P. M.

Special regulations for a shorter work-day on Saturdays.

In a Workshop which does not employ Children or Young People. (Sec. 29.)

The period of employment shall, except on Saturdays, be a specified period of twelve hours taken between 6 A. M. and 10 P. M.

There shall be allowed to a woman for meals and absence from work during the period of employment not less than one and one-half hours.

(*b*) FRANCE

The law of 1848, as amended by Act of November 2, 1892, and March 30, 1900, which became operative in 1904, provides in substance:

Hours of Labor (in industrial establishments).

The maximum length of the working day shall be ten hours (Art. 3, sec. 2), broken by at least one hour of rest. (Art. 3, sec. 1.)

Overtime may be granted by departmental decrees for two hours in one day, during not more than sixty days in the year, for certain trades, chiefly season trades. (Art. 4, sec. 4.) By departmental decrees employment of women may be prohibited or regulated in trades considered dangerous to health or morals. (Arts. 12 and 13.)

(c) Switzerland

The Canton of Glarus enacted in 1848 a law limiting the hours of labor to thirteen in one day. In 1864 this limit was reduced to twelve hours, and in 1872 it was further reduced to eleven hours. The Town of Basel enacted in 1869 a law limiting the hours of labor to twelve in one day.

The Canton of Ticino enacted in 1873 a law limiting the hours of labor to twelve in one day.

The Federal Swiss Constitution of 1874 provided:

Article 34: The Confederation has the right to make uniform prescription . . . concerning the duration of labor which may be required of adults.

The Federal law enacted in 1877 provides:

Hours of Labor (in industrial establishments).

The daily hours of work shall not exceed eleven hours in one day, and shall not exceed ten hours on the days before Sundays or holidays.

These working hours must be broken by a rest of at least one hour at noon; one and one-half hours for women who have to attend to household. (Art. 2, sec. 1.)

Overtime may be granted by the separate cantons for fixed times and fixed hours.

All the cantons have the same restriction of hours as is fixed by the Federal law except

Zurich (Law of 1894).

Hours of Labor (in industrial establishments).

The daily hours of labor shall not exceed ten hours in one day, and shall not exceed nine hours on the days before Sundays and holidays.

Overtime allowed for two hours in the day during seventy-five days in the year for various causes, such as season trades, press of work, etc. (Art. 9–16.)

(d) AUSTRIA

First law enacted in 1885; as amended by Acts of 1897, provides, in substance:

Hours of Labor (in factories and workshops).

Women shall not be employed more than eleven hours in one day. (Art. 96 a, secs. 1–3).

These working hours must be broken by rests amounting to one and one-half hours, one hour of which is allowed at noon. (Art. 74 a.)

Overtime for one hour in the day may be granted by the Ministers of Commerce and of the Interior for certain trades, the list of which must be revised every three years. (Art. 96 a, secs. 1–3.)

The Ministers may prohibit or regulate employment of women in trades held dangerous to health.

(e) HOLLAND

First law enacted in 1889 provides as follows:

Hours of Labor (in factories and workshops).

The daily hours of labor shall not exceed eleven hours in one day. (Art. 5, sec. 1.)

Between 11 A. M. and 3 P. M. a rest of at least one hour must be allowed. (Art. 6.)

Overtime may be granted by the provincial governors, allowing a thirteen-hour day for at most six consecutive days, or on alternative days during two weeks. (Art. 5, sec. 3.)

By royal decree employment of women may be prohibited or regulated in trades held dangerous to health.

(f) ITALY

The law of June 19, 1902, provides in substance:

Hours of Labor.

Women shall not be employed more than twelve hours in one day. (Art. 7.)

The day's work shall be broken by one or more rests amounting to one and one-half hours in a day of from eight to eleven hours, and amounting to two hours in a day of more than eleven hours. (Art. 8.)

(g) GERMANY

The law of 1891 provides in substance:

Hours of Labor (in industrial establishments).

Women shall not be employed more than eleven hours in one day, and not more than ten hours on the days before Sundays or holidays.

These working hours must be broken by a rest of at least one hour at noon, or one and one-half hours for women who have to attend to a household.

Overtime may be granted by the lower administrative authority for not more than thirteen hours of labor in one day, during two weeks, not more than forty days in the year. (Art. 138 a, secs. 1–3.)

In case of accidents the higher administrative authority may allow overtime without any restriction of hours during four weeks, the Chancellor of the Empire for any longer period. (Art. 139, sec. 1.)

The Bundesrat may grant overtime for special trades. (Art. 139 a, secs. 1 and 2.)

The Bundesrat may prohibit or regulate employment of women in trades held dangerous to health or morals. (Art. 139 a, sec. 1.)

II. THE AMERICAN LEGISLATION

Twenty States of the Union, including nearly all of those in which women are largely employed in factory or similar work, have found it necessary to take action for the protection of their health and safety and the public welfare, and have enacted laws limiting the hours of labor for adult women.

This legislation has not been the result of sudden impulse or passing humor, — it has followed deliberate consideration, and been adopted in the face of much opposition. More than a generation has elapsed between the earliest and the latest of these acts.

In no instance has any such law been repealed. Nearly every amendment in any law has been in the line of strengthening the law or further reducing the working time.

The earliest statute in the United States which undertook to limit the hours of labor for women in mechanical or manufacturing establishments was Wisconsin Statute, 1867, chap. 83, which fixed the hours of labor as eight. The act, however, provided a penalty only in case of compelling a woman to work longer hours.

See present Wisconsin Law, *supra*, p. 6.

The earliest act which effectively restricted the hours of labor for women was Massachusetts Statute, 1874, chap. 34, which fixed the limit at ten hours. The passage of the Massachusetts Act was preceded by prolonged agitation and repeated official investigations. The first legislative inquiry was made as early as 1865.

After the Massachusetts Act had been in force six years, an elaborate investigation of its economic effects was undertaken by the Massachusetts Bureau of Labor Statistics, under the supervision of its chief, Mr. Carroll D. Wright. His report, published in 1881 (Twelfth Annual Report of the Massachusetts Bureau of Statistics of Labor), to the effect that the reduction of the hours of labor had not resulted in increasing the cost or reducing wages, led to the passage, in 1885 and 1887, of the ten-hour law for women in Rhode Island, Maine, New Hampshire, and Connecticut, and largely influenced the legislation in other States.

See present laws, *supra*, pp. 1–8.

In the United States, as in foreign countries, there has been a general movement to strengthen and to extend the operation of these laws. In no State has any such law been held unconstitutional, except in Illinois, where, in Ritchie *v.* People, 154 Ill. 98, the Act of June 17, 1893, entitled "An Act to regulate the manufacture of clothing, wearing apparel, and other articles in this State," etc., was held unconstitutional. That act provided (sec. 5) that "No female shall be employed in any factory or workshop more than eight hours in any one day or forty-eight hours in any one week."

PART SECOND

THE WORLD'S EXPERIENCE UPON WHICH THE LEGISLATION LIMITING THE HOURS OF LABOR FOR WOMEN IS BASED

I. THE DANGERS OF LONG HOURS

A. *Causes*

(1) PHYSICAL DIFFERENCES BETWEEN MEN AND WOMEN

The dangers of long hours for women arise from their special physical organization taken in connection with the strain incident to factory and similar work.

Long hours of labor are dangerous for women primarily because of their special physical organization. In structure and function women are differentiated from men. Besides these anatomical and physiological differences, physicians are agreed that women are fundamentally weaker than men in all that makes for endurance: in muscular strength, in nervous energy, in the powers of persistent attention and application. Overwork, therefore, which strains endurance to the utmost, is more disastrous to the health of women than of men, and entails upon them more lasting injury.

Report of Select Committee on Shops Early Closing Bill, British House of Commons, 1895.

Dr. Percy Kidd, physician in Brompton and London Hospitals:

The most common effect I have noticed of the long hours is general deterioration of health; very general symptoms which we medi-

cally attribute to over-action, and debility of the nervous system; that
includes a great deal more than what is called nervous disease, such as
indigestion, constipation, a general slackness, and a great many other
indefinite symptoms.

Are those symptoms more marked in women than in men?

I think they are much more marked in women. I should say one
sees a great many more women of this class than men; but I have
seen precisely the same symptoms in men, I should not say in the same
proportion, because one has not been able to make anything like a
statistical inquiry. There are other symptoms, but I mention those
as being the most common. Another symptom especially among
women is anæmia, bloodlessness or pallor, that I have no doubt is
connected with long hours indoors. (Page 215.)

*Report of Committee on Early Closing of Shops Bill, British House of
Lords, 1901.*

Sir W. MacComac, President of the Royal College of Surgeons:

Would you draw a distinction between the evil resulting to women
and the evil resulting to men?

You see men have undoubtedly a greater degree of physical capacity than women have. Men are capable of greater effort in various
ways than women. If a like amount of physical toil and effort be
imposed upon women, they suffer to a larger degree. (Page 219.)

Report of the Maine Bureau of Industrial and Labor Statistics, 1888.

Let me quote from Dr. Ely Van der Warker (1875):

Woman is badly constructed for the purposes of standing eight
or ten hours upon her feet. I do not intend to bring into evidence the
peculiar position and nature of the organs contained in the pelvis,
but to call attention to the peculiar construction of the knee and the
shallowness of the pelvis, and the delicate nature of the foot as part
of a sustaining column. The knee joint of woman is a sexual char-
acteristic. Viewed in front and extended, the joint in but a slight
degree interrupts the gradual taper of the thigh into the leg. Viewed
in a semi-flexed position, the joint forms a smooth ovate spheroid.
The reason of this lies in the smallness of the patella in front, and the
narrowness of the articular surfaces of the tibia and femur, and
which in man form the lateral prominences, and thus is much more
perfect as a sustaining column than that of a woman. The muscles

which keep the body fixed upon the thighs in the erect position labor under the disadvantage of shortness of purchase, owing to the short distance, compared to that of man, between the crest of the ilium and the great trochanter of the femur, thus giving to man a much larger purchase in the leverage existing between the trunk and the extremities. Comparatively the foot is less able to sustain weight than that of man, owing to its shortness and the more delicate formation of the tarsus and metatarsus. (Page 142.)

Report of the Massachusetts Bureau of Labor Statistics, 1875.

A "lady operator," many years in the business, informed us: "I have had hundreds of lady compositors in my employ, and they all exhibited, in a marked manner, both in the way they performed their work and in its results, the difference in physical ability between themselves and men. They cannot endure the prolonged close attention and confinement which is a great part of type-setting. I have few girls with me more than two or three years at a time; they must have vacations, and they break down in health rapidly. I know no reason why a girl could not set as much type as a man, if she were as strong to endure the demand on mind and body." (Page 96.)

Report of the Nebraska Bureau of Labor and Industrial Statistics, 1901–1902.

They (women) are unable, by reason of their physical limitations, to endure the same hours of exhaustive labor as may be endured by adult males. Certain kinds of work which may be performed by men without injury to their health would wreck the constitution and destroy the health of women, and render them incapable of bearing their share of the burdens of the family and the home. The State must be accorded the right to guard and protect women as a class against such a condition, and the law in question to that extent conserves the public health and welfare. (Page 52.)

Hygiene of Occupations. By DR. THEODORE WEYL. *Jena, 1894.*

The investigations of Schuler and Burkhardt embracing 18,000 members of Swiss insurance against sickness (about 25 per cent of the Swiss factory workers and fifteen industries), show that factory work, even in a short period, produces very unfavorable effects upon the development of the body of young men. It is even more conspicuous in the case of women. Thus of 1000 men in the manufacture

of embroidery, 302 were sick to 332 women. In bleaching and dye-
ing, 279 men, 316 women; also in cotton spinning and weaving, the
morbidity of women was much greater than of men.

Similarly the number of working days lost through illness was
more among women than among men, being 6.47 among women to
6.25 among men.

With increasing years, both frequency and duration of illness
increase. (Page 7.)

A second form of physical inferiority of women is their lessened
refractoriness to external injurious conditions. All statistics dealing
with the relative morbidity of men and women employed in factories
justify the deduction that the greater number of days lost from work
by women indicate that disease makes greater inroads upon them,
and that in general industrial labor is more injurious to women than
to men. (Page 86.)

Travail de Nuit des Femmes dans l'Industrie. PROF. ETIENNE
BAUER. *Jena*, 1903.

From the point of view of hygiene the protection of wage-earning
women cannot fail to have good effects in view of the greater morbidity
of women. According to the statistics of the Krankenkassen of the
German Empire there occurred in each case where the patient is a
man 16.7 days of assistance rendered, or hospital treatment, and each
case of sickness where the patient is a woman, 18.6 days, in the period
1888–1899. (Page xxxvii.)

Man and Woman. HAVELOCK ELLIS.

In strength as well as in rapidity and precision of movement
women are inferior to men. This is not a conclusion that has ever
been contested. It is in harmony with all the practical experience of
life. It is perhaps also in harmony with the results of those investi-
gators (Bibra, Pagliani, etc. Arch. per l'Antrop., Vol. VI, p. 173) who
have found that, as in the blood of women, so also in their muscles,
there is more water than in those of men. To a very great extent it
is a certainty, a matter of difference in exercise and environment. It
is probably, also, partly a matter of organic constitution. (Page 155.)

The motor superiority of men, and to some extent of males generally, is, it can scarcely be doubted, a deep-lying fact. It is related
to what is most fundamental in men and in women, and to their whole
psychic organization. (Page 156.)

There appears to be a general agreement that women are more docile and amenable to discipline; that they can do light work equally well; that they are steadier in some respects; but that, on the other hand, they are often absent on account of slight indisposition, and they break down sooner under strain. (Page 183.)

History of Factory Legislation. HUTCHINS *and* HARRISON. 1903.

Women are "not only much less free agents than men," but they are physically incapable of bearing a continuance of work for the same length of time as men, and a deterioration of their health is attended with far more injurious consequences to society. (Page 84.)

Report of the British Chief Inspector of Factories and Workshops, 1903, on the Thirteenth International Congress of Hygiene and Demography.

Dr. Treves cited the case of a machine capable of giving 33,000 blows per diem, at which the men employed utilize on an average 18,000 to 20,000, while the women, less inured to fatigue and less capable of attention, utilize but 13,000.

Hygiene of Occupation in Reference Handbook of the Medical Sciences. GEORGE M. PRICE, M. D., *Medical Sanitary Inspector, Health Department of the City of New York.* Vol. VI.

In many industries . . . female labor is very largely employed; and the effect of work on them is very detrimental to health. The injurious influences of female labor are due to the following factors: (1) The comparative physical weakness of the female organism; (2) The greater predisposition to harmful and poisonous elements in the trades; (3) The periodical semi-pathological state of health of women; (4) The effect of labor on the reproductive organs; and (5) The effects on the offspring. As the muscular organism of woman is less developed than that of man, it is evident that those industrial occupations which require intense, constant, and prolonged muscular efforts must become highly detrimental to their health. This is shown in the general debility, anæmia, chlorosis, and lack of tone in most women who are compelled to work in factories and in shops for long periods.

The increased susceptibility of women to industrial poisons and to diseases has been demonstrated by a great number of observers. The female organism, especially when young, offers very little resistance to the inroads of disease and to the various dangerous elements of certain trades. Hirt says, "It must be conceded that certain trades affect women a great deal more injuriously than men;" and he mentions, among others, the effects of lead, mercury, phosphorus, and other poisons. Even where there are no special noxious elements, work may produce, as already mentioned, harmful effects on the health of women; but when to the general effects of industrial occupation are added the dangers of dust, fumes, and gases, we find that the female organism succumbs very readily, as compared with that of the male. Schuler found the frequency of sickness in females under eighteen, as compared with that of men of the same age is as 174 to 100. Miss Mary E. Abrams (Oliver: "Dangerous Trades") found that out of 138 lead-poisoning cases in Newcastle, where the number of men and women workers was about the same, there were ninety-four cases among the women and forty-one among the men. She also found that out of the twenty-three deaths from plumbism in the years 1889–1892, twenty-two were women and only one was a man. The women were all between seventeen and thirty years of age. These figures are substantiated by Hirt, Arlidge, C. Paul, Tardien, and others. The predisposition of women in industrial occupations to disease in general is greater than it is in men, as was proven by Hirt in his statistics of tuberculosis among workers. The effect of work on the physical development of women was found to be very detrimental, especially when they were very young. Arlidge says that in those who from their youth work in high temperatures, the bones and joints are imperfectly developed, and that they are liable to female deformities and to narrow pelves. Herkner found in his studies of Belgian female workers that girls who are engaged in mines suffered from deformed joints, from deformities of the spinal column, and from narrow pelves.

It has been estimated that out of every one hundred days women are in a semi-pathological state of health for from fourteen to sixteen days. The natural congestion of the pelvic organs during menstruation is augmented and favored by work on sewing-machines and other industrial occupations necessitating the constant use of the lower part of the body. Work during these periods tends to induce chronic congestion of the uterus and appendages, and dysmenorrhœa and flexion of the uterus are well known affections of working girls. (Page 321.)

(2) The New Strain in Manufacture

Such being their physical endowment, women are affected to a far greater degree than men by the growing strain of modern industry. Machinery is increasingly speeded up, the number of machines tended by individual workers grows larger, processes become more and more complex as more operations are performed simultaneously. All these ·changes involve correspondingly greater physical strain upon the worker.

Reports of Medical Commissioners on the Health of Factory Operatives Parliamentary Papers, 1833, Vol. XXI.

The first and most influential of all disadvantages of factory work is the indispensable, undeviating necessity of forcing both their mental and bodily exertions to keep exact pace with the motions of machinery propelled by unceasing, unvarying power. (Page 72.)

Factory and Workshop Act Commission, 1875. British Sessional Papers, 1876.

We have already referred more than once to the unremitting and monotonous character of all labor at a machine driven by steam. If the day's work of a housemaid or even of a charwoman be closely looked at and compared with that of an ordinary mill hand in a card room or spinning room, it will be seen that the former, though occasionally making greater muscular efforts than are ever exacted from the latter, is .yet continually changing both her occupation and her posture, and has very frequent intervals of rest. Work at a machine has inevitably a treadmill character about it; each step may be easy, but it must be performed at the exact moment under pain of consequences. In hand work and house work there is a certain freedom of doing or of leaving undone. Mill (*i. e.* machine) work must be done as if by clockwork. . . . The people are tied as it were to machinery moving at a great speed in certain operations; again it has been alleged that the state of the atmosphere is very unhealthy, and the temperature at a great height, and from the employment of machinery the speed has been so much increased, that the wear and tear, not merely of the body but of the mind also, of the operatives were too great for them to bear.

Report of the Maine Bureau of Industrial and Labor Statistics, 1892.

The constant nervous tension from continued exertion in a modern factory or workshop, for a period of ten hours, is a severe strain upon the physical system. Work is not done in the old, slow way, and, in nearly all industries, by the present methods, from two to four times the quantity of product is turned out in the ten hours. How much faster is the operative compelled to work, and how much greater is the strain, to accomplish this amount of work, in comparison with the old twelve-hour method. (Page 11.)

The Effect of Machinery on Wages. London, 1892.

The power of machinery is from one point of view too great and continuous — machines breathing fire and smoke, those slaves of iron and steel, as Cournot calls them, can go on night and day at high pressure. Hence results the tendency of machinery to add enormously to the toil of the laborers by increasing the day's labor both in length and intensity. Trades-unions often object to piece-work because, to use a rowing phrase, the best men set too fast a stroke for the comfort of the average workman, but the strength of the strongest is as water compared with the strength of machinery. This objection to machines has been forcibly stated by Chevalier: " Machinery imposes on man a crushing task. Feeble appendage of a mighty force, a tiny engine bound to an engine of immense power, the workman must bow to its attractions, give way to the rapidity of its movements, follow it in its incessant pace — in a word, he must turn, twist, and toil just as much as the untiring machinery pleases." (Pages 62, 63.)

The following from the *Cotton Factory Times*, February, 1892, illustrates very forcibly the influence of machinery in setting too fast a pace: " We have frequently heard spinners in cotton mills talk about being worked up, and made such that they could neither enjoy food nor rest and their lives felt a burden to them, and after leaving the mills at night they can be seen wending their way to places where they can quench their thirst, and liquids take precedence over food, which the appetite does not call for when the human system is overworked and overheated and the mind greatly disturbed by the difficulties and hardships which surround the workmen in their employments." (Page 74.)

Effects of the Factory System. *By* ALLEN CLARKE. *London,* 1899.

Greater speed of improved machinery, whereby the work is increased sixfold, resulting in physical deterioration and mental worry. (Page 41.)

The toil is ceaseless; the machinery demands constant watching. . . . Their feet are never still; their hands are full of tasks; their eyes are always on the watch; they toil in an unending strain that is cruel on the nerves. (Page 49.)

And all these hours — ten hours a day — spinner and weaver are on their feet; no sitting down; no resting; one must keep up to the machinery though agonized with headache or troubled by any other complaint. While the engine runs the workers must stand. (Page 51.)

Report of the United States Industrial Commission, 1900.

Mrs. Robertson tells me that when she was a girl, to run one or two looms was as much as any woman would have tried. Now, in some instances, there are women running nine looms, and the looms have more than doubled or trebled their speed. This means more work and harder work. (Page 63.)

Report of the United States Industrial Commission, 1901.

It is brought out that in nearly all occupations an increasing strain and intensity of labor is required by modern methods of production. . . . The introduction of machinery and the division of labor have made it possible to increase greatly the speed of the individual workman. . . . The testimony of a representative of the Cotton Weavers' Association shows this increasing strain of work. He says:

"Anybody who works in the mills now knows it is not like what it was twenty-five or thirty years ago, because the speed of the machinery has been increased to such an extent, and they have to keep up with it." (Page 763.)

Even these cases where machinery has not increased the intensity of exertion, a long workday with the machine, especially where work is greatly specialized, in many cases reduces the grade of intelligence. The old handwork shops were schools of debate and discussion, and they are so at the present time where they survive in country districts;

but the factory imposes silence and discipline for all except the highest. Long workdays under such conditions tend to inertia and dissipation when the day's work is done. (Page 772.)

Dangerous Trades. By THOMAS OLIVER, M. A., M. D., F. R. C. P.,
Medical Expert on the White Lead, Dangerous Trades, Pottery, and Lucifer Match Committees of the Home Office. London, 1902.

The introduction of steam has revolutionized industry. . . . Machinery acts with unerring uniformity. At times so simple is its mechanism that a child can almost guide it, yet how exacting are its demands. While machinery has in some senses lightened the burden of human toil, it has not diminished fatigue in man. All through the hours of work in a factory the hum of the wheels never ceases. . . . While the machinery pursues its relentless course and is insensitive to fatigue, human beings are conscious, especially towards the end of the day, that the competition is unequal, for their muscles are becoming tired and their brains jaded. . . . Present-day factory labor is too much a competition of sensitive human nerve and muscle against insensitive iron, and yet, apart from an appropriate shortening of the hours of labor, it is difficult to see how this can be remedied. The greater the number of hours machinery runs per day the larger is the output for the manufacturer, but the feebler are the human limbs that guide it. To the machine time is nothing; to the human being each hour that passes beyond a well-defined limit means increasing fatigue and exhaustion. (Page 117.)

The Working Hours of Female Factory Hands. From the Reports of Factory Inspectors, collated in the Imperial Home Office. Berlin, 1905.

From Frankfurt am Oder it is reported that the insurance records for two textile mills show steady deterioration in the health of the women employed eleven hours a day. One reason for this is believed to be the speeding up of the machinery. Vigorous weavers stated repeatedly that the old, slow looms exhausted them less in twelve and thirteen hours than the swift new looms in eleven hours. The more intensive work requires better nourishment; but there is no adequate increase in wages to afford this improved food, and the eleven-hour day of more rapid work is presumably responsible for the deteriorated health. (Page 119.)

B.   *Bad Effect of Long Hours on Health*

The fatigue which follows long hours of labor becomes chronic and results in general deterioration of health. Often ignored, since it does not result in immediate disease, this weakness and anæmia undermines the whole system; it destroys the nervous energy most necessary for steady work, and effectually predisposes to other illness. The long hours of standing, which are required in many industries, are universally denounced by physicians as the cause of pelvic disorders.

(1) General Injuries from Long Hours

Reports of Medical Commissioners on the Health of Factory Operatives. David Barry. *British Sessional Papers*, 1833, Vol. XXI.

Evidence of Francis Sharp, at Leeds, member of College of Surgeons in London, student of medical profession for fourteen years, house surgeon of Leeds Infirmary for four years:

" The nervous energy of the body I consider to be weakened by the very long hours, and a foundation laid for many diseases. . . . Were it not for the individuals who join the mills from the country, the factory people would soon be deteriorated." (Pages 12, 13.)

" Females whose work obliges them to stand constantly, are more subject to varicose veins of the lower extremities and to a larger and more dangerous extent than ever I have witnessed even in footsoldiers." (Page 73.)

Massachusetts Legislative Documents. House, 1866, No. 98.

(Specific) cases are not necessary to show the injurious effect of constant labor at long hours. . . . There may be serious evils from constant and exhausting labor, that do not show themselves in any positive, clearly defined disease; while nevertheless the vital forces of the whole man, physical and mental, are very greatly impaired. (Page 35.)

Dr. Jarvis, physician of Dorchester, says:

"Every man has a certain amount of constitutional force. This is his vital capital which must not be diminished. Out of this comes daily a certain and definite amount of available force, which he may expend in labor of muscle or brain, without drawing on his vital capital. He may and he should work every day and expend so much force and no more, that he shall awake the next morning and every succeeding morning until he shall be threescore and ten, and find in himself the same amount of available force, the same power, and do his ordinary day's work, and again lie down at night with his . . . constitutional force unimpaired."

Judging by this standard, there can be no doubt of the serious injury often resulting from overwork, even when no palpable evidence appears. (Page 36.)

Dr. Ordway, practising physician many years (in Lawrence), has no hesitation in saying that mill work, long continued, is injurious to bodily and mental health, and materially shortens life, especially of women. (Page 63.)

Reports of Commissioners on the Hours of Labor. Massachusetts Legislative Documents. House, 1867, No. 44.

Women are held under the present customs and ideas to at least five hours each half day of continuous work, often in the most tedious, minute, and monotonous employ. It is assumed . . . that they have no lower limbs to ache with swollen or ruptured veins, no delicacy of nerve, or versatility of mind, to revolt from such severity of application. (Page 66.)

Massachusetts Bureau of Statistics of Labor. Domestic Labor and Woman's Work, 1872.

In the cotton mills at Fitchburg the women and children are pale, crooked, and sickly-looking. The women appear dispirited, and the children without the bloom of childhood in their cheeks, or the elasticity that belongs to that age. Hours, 60 to 67¾ a week. (Page 94.)

Report of the British Chief Inspector of Factories and Workshops, 1873, Vol. XIX.

The house surgeon of a large hospital has stated that every year he had a large number of cases of pulmonary disease in girls, the origin of which he could distinctly trace to long and late hours in overcrowded and unhealthy workrooms. (Page 43.)

Factory and Workshops Act Commission, 1875. Miss A. E. Todd. Great Britain Sessional Papers, 1876, Vol. XXIX, Appendix D.

I would say that factory work is often, but not always, injurious to those engaged in it; country girls especially suffer from the close air and confinement; many of them fall into consumption or bad health of some kind. I have known many deaths from this cause in this class. I have also found much derangement of the liver, stomach, and digestive organs, owing, I think, partially to the rapidity with which they are obliged to eat their meals. (Page 164.)

Report of the Maine Bureau of Industrial and Labor Statistics, 1888.

Many saleswomen are so worn out, when their week's work is ended, that a good part of their Sundays is spent in bed, recuperating for the next week's demands. And one by one girls drop out and die, often from sheer overwork. This I know from observation and personal acquaintance. (Page 142.)

Report of the British Chief Inspector of Factories and Workshops, 1893.

Arguments against overtime (*i. e.* more than ten and a half hours):

2. That the long hours of confinement are injurious to the health of the workers. . . .

"Overtime (*i. e.* over ten and a half hours daily) allows but scanty opportunity for leisure. . . . The consequent effect upon the health of the workers is exceedingly injurious. Some employers, too, hold that in proportion as the workpeople suffer in health, their work suffers in execution." (Page 11.)

Report of Select Committee on Shops Early Closing Bill, British House of Commons, 1895.

Miss MacDonald, M.B., now attached to the Hospital for Women in Euston Road:

Dr. Kidd told us just now that in his experience at Brompton Hospital there was a good deal of general deterioration of health among women?

That is exactly what I should say, anæmia and general nervous debility.

And would not standing so long very much affect women, if they were married, afterwards?

It is not good for women to stand . . . at all really.

If it is not good for them to stand at all, still less will it be good for them to stand thirteen hours a day?

I think it is shocking.

. . . The standing of course would exhaust the women and make them more liable to other illnesses. (See pages 5379–5387.)

Reports from Committee on Early Closing of Shops, British House of Lords, 1901, Vol. VI.

Considering the weight which belongs to that memorial (submitted by some doctors in 1888), the Committee did not deem it necessary to multiply medical evidence on the subject. The presidents, however, both of the College of Physicians and of the College of Surgeons, have come before us and spoken strongly on the great and increasing evils of the present long hours. Sir W. MacCormac stated that "There is no doubt in my mind that such long hours (it speaks of an average of fourteen hours per day) must contribute to the incidence of disease; that it must lower the general vitality of persons so engaged and render them more liable than they otherwise would be to attacks of different forms of disease. These hours, too, for the most part, are worked in an atmosphere very prejudicial to health, and we know how largely the air so contaminated contributed to the production of various forms of disease in which tubercule, for instance, and manifold forms of disease in which tubercule manifests itself, and that other disease of great cities (rickette) has some parts of its origin from this cause."

Furthermore, he urged on us that the evil is one which increases as time runs on; "it is gradual and progressive in its effects, and it goes on, I am afraid, in a cumulative degree."

Sir W. Selby Church, the president of the College of Physicians, gave similar evidence.

We are able, however, to appeal to the highest medical testimony as to the injury thus caused (long hours — especially on women).

In 1888 presidents of the two great medical colleges with some of the other leaders of the medical profession, Sir James Paget, Sir Andrew Clark, Dr. Matthews Duncan, Mr. John Marshall, Dr. Playfair, Dr. Priestly, Sir Richard Quain, Sir Wm. Savory, Sir Samuel Wilks, called the attention of Parliament to the subject and urged the passing of the Early Closing Bill. (Page v.)

Report of British Chief Inspectors of Factories and Workshops, 1901.

Ten and a half hours sitting bent over stitching, requiring very careful attention, with two intervals so short that only a hasty meal can be eaten, that there is no time for exercise, even were the workers permitted to go out, and that, day after day, might well'try the strongest constitutions and ruin the best digestions and nerves.

That its effect on the health is injurious is constantly brought before one, and anæmic and heavy-eyed workers who suffer from neuralgia who form too large a proportion of the whole number, make one feel very strongly that some reform is needed. (Page 176.)

Report of British Chief Inspector of Factories and Workshops, 1903. T. M. LEGGE, *H. M. Medical Inspector of Factories and Workshops.*

"A point of some importance which was mentioned to me by the medical attendant at one factory (cigar) was that the number of cases under treatment for sickness varied *pari passu* with the amount of overtime work," *i. e.* over ten hours in one day. (Page 286.)

Journal of Royal Sanitary Institute, Vol. XXV. M. G. BOND-FIELD. *London*, 1904.

Sir William MacCormac, giving evidence before the Lords' Committee on The Early Closing of Shops, said, "There is no doubt, I think in my mind, that such long hours must contribute to the incidence of disease; that it must lower the general vitality of persons so engaged, and render them more liable than they otherwise would be to attacks of different forms of disease. . . . These hours, too, for the most part are worked in an atmosphere very prejudicial to health. . . . I quite agree with the opinions of my predecessors that such long hours are very grievous, and are calculated to do the community in which they prevail serious harm. . . . It must have an influence on their offspring, undoubtedly. . . . In one sense it cannot be said to be urgent, but it is insidious; it is gradual and progressive in its effect. And it goes on I am afraid, in a cumulative degree." (Page 742.)

Sir William Church, who gave evidence the same day, said: "There is another great group which falls under the observation of the ordinary physician and of which we see a very great deal in our London Hospitals, and that is an anæmic condition which is produced partly by long hours of work, and still more by the confinement that this employment entails." (Page 743.)

From the Reports of Factory Inspectors. Collated in the Imperial Home Office, Berlin, 1905. The Working Hours of Female Factory Hands.

Report for Bremen: The reduction for the working hours for women will be of great value to the entire working population, and more especially to workingmen's families. It is of great hygienic importance on account of the more delicate physical organization of woman, and will contribute much toward the better care of children and the maintenance of a regular family life.

The Inspector for Erfurt urges the introduction of the ten-hour day for women because "eleven hours daily toil in a factory is extremely exhausting for the weaker physical organization of woman. Although perhaps under good sanitary conditions of work no direct injury to health may be traced to the eleven-hours day, still it is certain that women and girls who work in factories are worn out much sooner than those who do not. The factory worker who has most likely a poor physical inheritance to contend with, and is poorly nourished, is liable to frequent attacks of sickness."

Report for Cassel: The ill effects of factory work for women is most marked in those cases where long hours are joined to heavy work. The female frame is not strong enough to resist the harmful influence of such work for any length of time. Although the ill effects may not show themselves at once, it is not unlikely that injuries to health which manifest themselves years after may be traced back to former work in the factory. The total exclusion of women from the factories is not at present contemplated, but the introduction of the ten-hour day will tend towards reducing the harmful influence of factory work. (Page 107.)

The inspector for Erfurt reports that when a working girl marries, unless she is very strong she gradually fails in health and is frequently unfitted for giving birth to healthy children or to nurse those who are born. (Page 111.)

Report of the British Chief Inspector of Factories and Workshops, 1906. Appendix II. Report on Tobacco, Cigars and Cigarette Industry.

The question of the health of the workers has been the main object of our enquiry, and we have therefore given our attention chiefly to this point. It is impossible to consider the industry an unhealthy one. With the exception of one or two processes there has been little or no evidence to prove that the manufacture of tobacco is in itself injurious to health. . . . In six of the largest factories visited a very complete system of preliminary medical examination was found to be carried out by the doctors specially appointed by the firms. . . . We have gained a great deal of information from these doctors, whose experience is almost unique. Our attention was drawn to a very interesting and important point by two of the doctors; their experience (which in one case has been tabulated) had led them to form the opinion that overtime has a very marked bearing on the normal health of the workers. They had noted an increase during and just after periods of overtime work of from one-third to one-half in the number of workers coming to them for treatment; the matters complained of were not anything special, but simply an increase in the usual form of ailment, such as indigestion, anæmia, heavy colds (in winter), gastric disorders in summer. When one considers that overtime here means simply employment up to the normal legal period, that is, ten and ten and a half hours a day, and does not mean overtime as permitted in a large number of industries (in the case of women over eighteen), and which extends to twelve hours in the day, the result is all the more striking, and one feels that a similar record in one of the industries in which overtime is allowed would produce more noticeable statistics of the results of over-fatigue. The conclusion seems to us clear that eight and a half to nine hours' work a day cannot be exceeded by women and girls without overstrain and fatigue resulting in a lower standard of health. (Page 253.)

From Reports by the District Inspectors (of France) upon the Question of Night Work (Paris, 1900). By M. LEGARD, *Inspecteur Divisionnaire de la* 10e *circonscription à Marseille.*

During an investigation made by the inspector (lady) of work in the dressmaking establishments of the city of Marseilles, several workingwomen complained that after a certain number of evenings of overtime, they did not recover their sleep, dispelled by fatigue. They went home to sleep some hours in the morning before returning to their work. Therefore these workers lost a part of the seven or eight hours of sleep absolutely requisite to an adult for proper rest. They did not have restful nights after very full days. Insomnia visited them with all its accompanying evils. Sleep is so important from the health standpoint that there is perhaps no function which should be so conscientiously exercised. Everything which affects the hygiene of sleep constitutes a danger, because the equilibrium of the nervous system is jeopardized. (Page 71.)

Age and Sex in Occupations. Twentieth Century Practice of Medicine,
1895, Vol. III. *By* Dr. James H. Lloyd.

Woman may suffer in health in various ways that do not affect
materially her mortality — neurasthenia, the bane of overworked and
underfed women, does not leave a definite trace on the mortality tables.

Again, woman's ill-health and drudgery in a factory may affect her
progeny in a way that the statistician cannot estimate. (Page 326.)

Women are said to suffer from derangements and displacements
from occupations requiring long standing and certain movements of
the body, while the lacteal secretion is impaired by some occupations,
and also by enforced absence of mothers from their nursing infants.
(Page 327).

Neurasthenia from overwork. . . . It cannot be ignored, because
among its well recognized and active causes is the strain of excessive
labor. (Page 488).

I have been struck . . . with the numerous facts that have come
to my notice tending to convince me that one of the most common
effects of overwork and poor hygiene in industrial life is an ill-defined
condition of neurasthenia, insomnia, headache, and pains in and along
the spine . . . extreme lassitude and weakness occur.

The treatment of neurasthenia from overwork should be first, by re-
moving or modifying the cause as much as possible. (Page 490.)

Journal of the American Medical Association, May 19, 1906. *Fatigue.*
By Dr. Frederick S. Lee, *Prof. Physiology, Columbia University, N. Y.*

There are probably few physiologic functions that are not affected
unfavorably by the prolonged and excessive activity of the muscular
and the nervous systems. In such a condition the normal action of
the tissues may easily give place to pathologic action.

Fatigue undoubtedly diminishes the resistance of the tissues to
bacteria, and also predisposes the individual to attacks from diseases
other than bacterial. . . .

Heretofore attention has been directed chiefly to the extreme effects
of the pathologic acids. . . .

We should not forget, however, that long before these extreme
effects are manifested the same causes are producing evil, if less
obvious, phenomena, and rendering the cells less capable of their
proper functions. . . .

Mankind at present can administer no food or drug that can push
the wearied cells up the metabolic grade. . . . Only the assimilation

and ditoxication that normally come with rest, and best, rest with sleep, are capable of adequate restoring power.

The Hygiene, Diseases, and Mortality of Occupations. 1892. J. T. ARLIDGE, M. D., F. R. C. P., *Late Melroy Lecturer at Royal College.*

Excessive exertion may operate either over a long period and produce its ill results slowly, or be sudden and severe. . . . When such people are seized by some definite lesion, attention is so completely attracted to it that the antecedent over-toil laying the foundation for the malady is apt to be overlooked. (Page 16.)

The want of exercise of the body induces general torpidity of functions, reduces lung capacity and respiratory completeness, and the activity of the abdominal muscles, which aid both respiration and the functions of the digestive organs. Hence, the proclivity to venous stasis (congestion), particularly in the pelvis and lower extremities and in the rectal vessels, with the production of constipation, — and in women of menstrual difficulties, — add to these disorders of digestion in their multiform shape, debilitated muscular power, and a low vitality and vigor generally.

When insufficient muscular activity is associated with almost constant standing, the increased difficulty to the return of the blood from the lower limbs is the most pronounced feature, and productive of varicose veins, and ulcers and thickened knee, and ankle joints. (Page 19.)

(2) SPECIFIC EVIL EFFECTS ON CHILDBIRTH AND FEMALE FUNCTIONS

The evil effect of overwork before as well as after marriage upon childbirth is marked and disastrous.

Report of Select Committee on Shops Early Closing Bill. British House of Commons, 1895.

Testimony of Dr. W. Chapman Grigg (formerly out-patient physician for the diseases of women at Westminster Hospital, and senior physician to the Queen Charlotte Lying-in Hospital and the Victoria Hospital for Children).

Would you please tell us in a general way your experience as to the effects of these prolonged hours on health?

It has a very grave effect upon the generative organs of women, entailing a great deal of suffering and also injuring a very large body of them permanently, setting up inflammation in the pelvis in connection with those organs. . . .

I have had a great many sad cases come before me of women who were permanent invalids in consequence.

If the matter could be gone into carefully, I think the committee would be perfectly surprised to find what a large number of these women are rendered sterile in consequence of these prolonged hours.

I believe that is one of the greatest evils attached to these prolonged hours. I have seen many cases in families where certain members who have pursued the calling of shop-girl assistants have been sterile, while other members of the family have borne children. I know of one case where four members of a family who were shop-girls were sterile, and two other girls in the family, not shop-girls, have borne children; and I have known other cases in which this has occurred. . . . I have patients come to me from all parts of London. It appears to be a most common condition.

When these women have children, do you find that the children themselves suffer from the woman having been affected by these very long hours?

I have seen many cases where I have attributed the mischief arising in childbed to this inflammatory mischief in the mother, which, after delivery, has set up fresh mischief, and I have seen serious consequences resulting. (Page 219.)

Report to the Local Governing Board on Proposed Changes in Hours and Ages of Employment in Textile Factories, by J. H. BRIDGES, M.D., *and* T. HOLMES. *British Parliamentary Papers.* 1873. Vol. LV. (Page 39.)

Experience afforded by residence in the worsted manufacturing town of Bradford, and extensive practise among its population during periods of from one to thirty-five years:

A. Amongst the *women* of factory operatives, much more than among the general population, derangements of the digestive organs are common, *e. g.*, pyrosis, sickness, constipation, vertigo, and headache, generated by neglect of the calls of nature through the early hours of work, the short intervals at meals, the eating and drinking of easily prepared foods, as bread, tea, and coffee, and the neglect of meat and fresh cooked vegetables. Other deranged states of a still worse character are present, *e. g.*, leucorrhœa and too frequent and profuse

menstruation.   Cases also of displacement, flexions, and versions of
the uterus, arising from the constant standing and the increased heat
of and confinement in the mill. . . . Œdema and varicose veins of the
legs are common amongst female mill-workers of middle age.

Q. Has the labor any tendency to increase the rate of infant
mortality ?

A. Yes.   The evils occurring in women as detailed in answer to
question 2 indirectly affect the more perfect growth of the child in
utero, and dispose it when born more easily to become diseased.

Signed on behalf of the Bradford Medico Chirurgical Society, at a
meeting held February 4, 1873.

Sub-Committee.

President,   J. H. BELL, M.D.

P. E. MIALL, M.R.C.S.

Secretary,   DAVID GOYDER, M.D.

Report of the British Chief Inspector of Factories and Workshops,
1873. DR. R.H. LEACH, *Certifying Surgeon for over Thirty Years.*

Shorten their hours of labor, for I believe that scores of infants are
annually lost under the present system.   As things now stand, a
mother leaves her infant (say of two months old) at 6 A. M., often
asleep in bed, at 8 she nurses it, then until 12.30 the child is bottle fed,
or stuffed with indigestible food.   On her return at noon, overheated
and exhausted, her milk is unfit for the child's nourishment, and this
state of things is again repeated until 6 P. M.; the consequence is, that
the child suffers from spasmodic diarrhœa, often complicated with
convulsions and ending in death.

Report of Massachusetts Bureau of Labor Statistics, 1875.

It seems to be the back that gives out.   Girls cannot work more
than eight hours, and keep it up; they know it, and they rarely will, —
and even this seems to "pull them down," so that it is extremely rare
that a girl continues more than a few years at the business.

Mr. B——, foreman of a large printing establishment, says:
"Girls must sit at the 'case.'   I never knew but one woman, and she
a strong, vigorous Irishwoman, of unusual height, who could stand
at the case like a man.   Female compositors, as a rule, are sickly,
suffering much from backache, headache, weak limbs, and general
'female weakness.'"

Miss ——, for several years in charge of the female department of one of the largest offices in the country, testified: "One year is as long as one can work in a busy office without a good vacation. The confined position, constipation, heat, and dizzy headache, I think, are the most noticeable troubles of 'lady operators' who are 'grown up.' The hours are too long for such strained employment. From 8 A. M. to 6 P. M., with only an hour for dinner, makes too long a day for the kind of work." (Pages 90–92.)

Miss J——, a lady compositor, says: "We cannot stand at the 'case.' It increases back and head ache, and weakness of limbs, as well as a dragging weight about the hips. I have been at this work five years, but have been frequently obliged to give up for vacations from peculiar troubles and general debility. I began to menstruate when fourteen; I am now twenty-two. I was well until I had set type for a year, when I began to be troubled with difficult periods, and have been more or less ever since. When I go away I get better, but, as often as I return to my work, I am troubled again. Have wholly lost color, and am not nearly as fleshy and heavy as when I began work. I have now a good deal of pain in my chest, and some cough, which increases, if I work harder than usual. I am well acquainted with many other lady compositors who suffer as I do."

Miss S——, a lady long in charge of the "composing-room" (female department) of a large printing establishment testifies: "I was myself a compositor, and have had scores of girls under me and with me, many of whom I have known intimately. I have no hesitation in saying that I think I never knew a dozen lady compositors who were 'well.' Their principal troubles are those belonging to the sex, and great pain in back, limbs, and head."

Report of the Massachusetts Bureau of Statistics of Labor, 1884.

We secured the personal history of these 1032 of the whole 20,000 working girls of Boston, a number amply sufficient for the scientific purposes of the investigation. (Page 5.)

Long hours, and being obliged to stand all day, are very generally advanced as the principal reasons for any lack or loss of health occasioned by the work of the girls. 3. Exhaustion from overwork. In consequence of the long hours of labor, the great speed the machinery is run at, the large number of looms the weavers tend, and the general overtasking, so much exhaustion is produced in most cases that, immediately after taking supper, the tired operatives drop to sleep in their chairs. . . . 10. Predisposition to pelvic disease. There appears, as far as my observation goes, quite a predisposition to pelvic disease among the female factory operatives, producing difficulty in parturition. The necessity for instrumental delivery has very much increased within a few years, owing to the females working in the mills while they are pregnant and in consequence of deformed pelvis. Other uterine diseases are produced, and, in other cases, aggravated in consequence of the same. (Page 69.)

Report of the California Bureau of Labor Statistics, 1887–1888.

Dr. F. B. Kane of San Francisco says: "Very many times my attention has been drawn professionally to the injury caused by the long hours of standing required of the saleswomen in this city, the one position most calculated to cause the manifold diseases peculiar to their sex, and direfully does Nature punish the disobedience of her laws."

Dr. C. A. Clinton, of the San Francisco Board of Health, says: "I am decidedly of the opinion that it is highly injurious. It will certainly aggravate any existing complaints, and still more, it will and does have a tendency to induce complaints in persons previously free from them. It is especially injurious to females in regard to the diseases peculiar to the female sex." (Page 102.)

Report of the New Jersey Bureau of Statistics of Labor and Industries, 1902.

The weak, physical condition of the operatives, especially the females, is very noticeable. . . .

The long hours of labor, frequently ten or twelve, and the foul air of the workroom is most marked in its effects upon the female operatives. In addition to throat and lung diseases, which are almost equally prevalent among both sexes, the sufferings of the female operatives from causes peculiar to the sex is very greatly aggravated by the conditions under which they work.

A physician of high standing whose practice is largely among the operatives of these mills is authority for the statement that a large majority of female mill-workers are sufferers from some one or more of the organic complaints brought on or intensified by the conditions under which they work. If no such disease existed before entering the mill, it was almost sure to develop soon after beginning work; if it did exist before, it was aggravated to a degree that made them easy victims of consumption.

The long hours of labor, being constantly standing, the foul air of the workroom, and, more than all, the ceaseless vibration of the floor from the motion of the great mass of machinery are the prime factors in producing these diseases. (Page 377.)

La Réglémentation Légale du Travail des Femmes et des Enfants dans l'Industrie Italienne. LIONEL BAUDOIN.

At the International Congress at Milan, on accidents among the laboring class, in May, 1894, Mr. Luigi Belloc (Factory Inspector of the Department of Labor) represented Italy. He stated that the continuous motion of the body taxes the nervous system, causing the gravest troubles. The sewing-machine, which requires of the operator 40,000 movements a day, causes in the long run abdominal and renal troubles, disarrangement of the menstrual function, and falling and deviations of the uterus. Functional weaknesses and paralysis are the result of the continual performance of the same movement. The necessity of standing or sitting for the whole day causes malformation of the body or curvature of the spine, as a result of the strained position. The attention required in watching a machine, especially an automatic one, is very fatiguing, on account of the large number of wheels operating at the same time which need attention.

Women employed in the manufacture of tobacco and of matches are subject to gastric, intestinal troubles, and affections of the respiratory tract, necrosis of the jaw, and are liable to miscarriage. Women employed in sorting rags used in the manufacture of paper are liable to smallpox or carbuncle. Tuberculosis spreads with alarming rapidity, especially among cotton and wool weavers. Those whom tuberculosis spares drag along with anæmia, the most common malady of the women factory workers, especially the textile workers, who are subject to long hours of labor. . . .

For the cotton industry in particular Mr. Luigi Belloc demands the ten-hour day. (Page 14.)

Infant Mortality: A Social Problem. GEO. NEWMAN, M. D., *London*, 1906.

Physical fatigue, particularly if accompanied by a strain and stress, are likely to exert a decided effect in the production of premature birth, particularly if these conditions are accompanied by long hours of work and poor or insufficient nourishment. (Page 80.)

The direct injuries to women and girls employed in factories and workshops are: (c) Injury through fatigue and strain, long hours and insufficient periods of rest for food, . . . and (e) Too short a period of rest at the time of childbirth.

Over and over again, in the official reports of factory inspectors or medical officers of health, does one meet with evidences of these injuries. Where the conditions resulting in these evils, coupled with the absence of the mother from home, are present, the infant mortality is high; where they are not present, it is usually low. (Page 131.)

In consequence of the fact that while there has been a steady and continuous decline in the general mortality of Preston during the past thirty years, the infant mortality has shown an increase, a subcommittee was appointed to inquire into the causes (1902), and submitted certain conclusions:

(1) First among these causes is the employment of female labor in mills. An occupation requiring a woman to stand during the greater part of the day when continued up to within a few days or even hours of the time of parturition, must act to the detriment of the offspring, and there is less chance of the latter coming into the world fully grown, well formed, and in good health. Many deaths taking place during the first month, which are returned as due to premature birth, immaturity, congenital debility, convulsions, and the like, may safely be ascribed to this cause.

In a general way it may be said that it is the employment of women from girlhood all through married life and through the period of childbearing, the continual stress and strain of the work and hours, and general conditions prevailing in women's labor, that is exerting its baneful influence on the individual and on the home. (Page 134.)

C. Bad Effect of Long Hours on Safety

Accidents to working women occur most frequently at the close of the day, or after a long period of uninterrupted work. The coincidence of casualties and fatigue due to long hours is thus made manifest.

British Parliamentary Debates. Third Series. 1844. Vol. LXXIII. Lord Ashley's Speech.

"Those honourable gentlemen who have been in the habit of perusing the melancholy details of mill accidents should know that

a large proportion of those accidents — particularly those which
may be denominated the minor class, such as loss of fingers and the
like — occur in the last hours of the evening, when the people become
so tired that they absolutely get reckless of the danger. I state this
on the authority of several practical spinners. Hence arise many
serious evils to the working classes, none greater than the early
prostration of their strength." (Page 1082.)

Report of the German Imperial Factory Inspectors, 1895.

The ten-hour day, with the exceptions necessary for certain trades,
is a measure which can be introduced without great difficulty, and
which would prevent many dangers threatening the health of workers.
Many accidents are no doubt due to the relaxed vigilance and lessening
of bodily strength following excessive hours of work. (Page 369.)

Report of the British Chief Inspector of Factories and Workshops, 1900.

One can only feel surprise that accidents are not more numerous
(in laundries), when one realizes that the slightest carelessness or
inattention may result in the fingers or hand being drawn between
the hot cylinders, and when one considers how easily such inattention
may arise in the case of the over-tired young workers. (Page 383.)

Report of British Chief Inspector of Factories and Workshops, 1903.

The comparative immunity from accidents in the laundries in
the West Riding of Yorkshire may be possibly due in some measure
to the moderate hours of employment.

The incidents of accidents according to time of day is somewhat
surprising, the most dangerous hours apparently being 11 A. M. to
12 noon and 4 to 6 P. M. . . . Probably 11 A. M. to 12 noon is more
generally than any other time the last tiring hour of a day five hours'
spell; 4–6 P. M. covers the time when most generally the transition is
from daylight to artificial light. (Page 210.)

Reference was also made (in the Thirteenth International Congress
of Hygiene), although figures were not adduced, to the alleged increase
in the number of accidents which occur late in the working day when
the effect of intellectual and physical fatigue have made themselves
apparent. (Page 298.)

Infant Mortality: A Social Problem. GEORGE NEWMAN, M. D.,
London, 1906.

The results of fatigue become manifest in various ways, not the
least being the occurrence of accidents or of physical breakdown.
The former, as is now well recognized, occur most frequently in
fatigued workers. For example, since 1900 there has been a steady,
though not marked, increase in the number of accidents to women
over eighteen years of age in laundries. In 1900 such accidents
numbered 131; in 1904, 157. Now it has been shown that whilst
the first half of the day yields about the same number of accidents
as the second half, more accidents, amounting to nearly double the
number, occur between the hours of 11 A. M. and 1 P. M., and
between 4 P. M. and 7 P. M. than at any other time of the day.
(Page 112.)

Getting a Living. *By* G. L. BOHN.

CHAP. 15. SHORTER WORKDAY.

If in the tenth hour as much work has been done as the average
for the previous nine hours, a reduction of time to nine hours per
day, at the same pay, would be an increase of wages by eleven and
one-ninth per cent, unless the extra hour of rest increased the
hourly product. But in any work not fixed in speed by steadily
running machinery, less is done in the tenth hour, by reason of
weariness, than in other hours; and the work of the last hour,
like overtime work at night, weakens a person for the next day.
It is this weariness that causes accidents to occur two or three
times as frequently in the last hour as in other hours — a fact
proved by European statistics. With the steady machinery, too,
weariness, as a rule, either lowers the quality of the work done,
or by frequent stoppage lessens its amount — often causing both
these losses. (Page 407.)

D. *Bad Effect of Long Hours on Morals*

The effect of overwork on morals is closely related to
the injury to health. Laxity of moral fibre follows physical
debility. When the working day is so long that no time
whatever is left for a minimum of leisure or home-life,
relief from the strain of work is sought in alcoholic stimulants and other excesses.

Massachusetts Legislative Document.   House, 1866, No. 98.

Overwork is the fruitful source of innumerable evils.   Ten and eleven hours daily of hard labor are more than the human system can bear, save in a few exceptional cases. . . . It cripples the body, ruins health, shortens life.   It stunts the mind, gives no time for culture, no opportunity for reading, study, or mental improvement.   It leaves the system jaded and worn, with no ability to study. . . . It tends to dissipation in various forms.   The exhausted system craves stimulants.   This opens the door to other indulgences, from which flow not only the degeneracy of individuals, but the degeneracy of the race.   (Page 24.)

Relations between Labor and Capital.   U. S. Senate Committee, 1883.
   Vol. I.   *Testimony of* ROBERT HOWARD, *Mule-Spinner in Fall River Cotton Mills.*

I have noticed that the hard, slavish overwork is driving those girls into the saloons, after they leave the mills evenings . . . good, respectable girls, but they come out so tired and so thirsty and so exhausted . . . from working along steadily from hour to hour and breathing the noxious effluvia from the grease and other ingredients used in the mill.

Wherever you go . . . near the abodes of people who are overworked, you will always find the sign of the rum-shop.

Drinking is most prevalent among working people where the hours of labor are long.   (Page 647.)

The Case for the Factory Acts.   Edited by MRS. SIDNEY WEBB.
   London, 1901.

If working long and irregular hours, accepting a bare subsistence wage and enduring insanitary conditions tended to increase women's physical strength and industrial skill — if these conditions of unregulated industry even left unimpaired the woman's natural stock of strength and skill — we might regard factory legislation as irrelevant.   But as a matter of fact a whole century of evidence proves exactly the contrary.   To leave women's labor unregulated by law means inevitably to leave it exposed to terribly deteriorating influences.   The woman's lack of skill and lack of strength is made worse by lack of regulation.   And there is still a further deterioration.   Any one who has read the evidence given in the various inquiries into the Sweating System will have been struck by the invariable coincidence of a low standard of regularity, sobriety, and morality, with the conditions to which women, under free competition, are exposed. (Page 209.)

Dangerous Trades. THOMAS OLIVER, M. D. *London*, 1902.

It is frequently asserted that laundry women as a class are intemperate and rougher than most industrial workers. That they are peculiarly irregular in their habits it is impossible to deny; and the long hours, the discomfort and exhaustion due to constant standing in wet and heat, discourage the entrance into the trade of a better class of workers is certain. . . . The prevalence of the drink habit among many of them, of which so much is said, is not difficult to account for: the heat of an atmosphere often laden with particles of soda, ammonia, and other chemicals has a remarkably thirst-inducing effect; the work is for the most part exhausting, even apart from the conditions, and the pernicious habit of quenching the thirst, and stimulating an overtired physical condition, with beer. (Page 672.)

Report of the British Chief Inspector of Factories and Workshops, 1902.

The result is disastrous, even from the point of view of this industry itself, which if properly organized would be capable of offering really desirable employment to skilled workers instead of being, as it too often is, the last resort of the idle and intemperate. . . . I would add that too often the very intemperance is created by the conditions of employment, by the excessive overstrain of endurance. (Page 174.)

Report of the British Association for the Advancement of Science: the Economic Effect of Legislation Regulating Women's Labor, 1902.

On the morals of the workers there has been a marked effect [by the Factory Acts]. "Saint Monday" is now a thing of the past, and just as irregularity conduces to drunkenness and irregular living, and the rush of overtime at the end of the week, with nothing to do in the early parts, induced an irregular and careless mode of life, so the comparative steadiness of the present methods have tended to raise the standard of morality and sobriety. (Page 287.)

E. *Bad Effect of Long Hours on General Welfare*

The experience of manufacturing countries has illustrated the evil effect of overwork upon the general welfare. Deterioration of any large portion of the population inevitably lowers the entire community physically, mentally, and morally. When the health of women has been injured by long hours, not only is the working efficiency of the community impaired, but the deterioration is handed down to succeeding generations. Infant mortality rises, while the children of married working-women, who survive, are injured by inevitable neglect. The overwork of future mothers thus directly attacks the welfare of the nation.

(1) THE STATE'S NEED OF PROTECTING WOMAN

Report of the Massachusetts State Board of Health, 1873. EDWARD JARVIS, M. D.

All additions to the physical, moral, or intellectual power of individuals — in any individual are, to that extent, additions to the energy and the productive force — the effectiveness of the State; and on the contrary, all deductions from these forces, whether of mind or body — every sickness, and injury or disability, every impairment of energy — take so much from the mental force, the safe administration of the body politic. . . .

The State thus has an interest not only in the prosperity, but also in the health and strength and effective power of each one of its members. . . .

The first and largest interest of the State lies in the great agency of human power — the health of the people. (Page 336.)

Report of the Massachusetts Bureau of Labor Statistics, 1871.

It is claimed that legislation on this subject is an interference between labor and capital. . . . But legislation has interfered with capital and labor both, in the demand for public safety and the public good. Now public safety and public good, the wealth of the commonwealth, centred, as such wealth is, in the well-being of its common people, demands that the State should interfere by special act in favor of . . . working-women, and working children, by enacting a ten-hour law, to be enforced by a system of efficient inspection. (Page 567.)

International Conference in Relation to Labor Legislation. Berlin, 1890.

It is the idea of the German Emperor that the industrial question demands the attention of all the civilized nations. . . .

The quest of a solution becomes not only a humanitarian duty, but it is exacted also by governmental wisdom, which should at once look out for the well-being of all its citizens and the preservation of the inestimable benefits of civilization. (Page 29.)

Proceedings of the French Senate. Session of July 7, 1891. M. JULES SIMON.

It is impossible for me not to tell the Senate what I think of the position of women in industry, and that I may gain your favor, gentlemen, I ask permission to tell you that for at least forty years I have applied myself to this question. (Page 573.)

When I ask, when we ask, for a lessening of the daily toil of women, it is not only of the women that we think; it is not principally of the women, it is of the whole human race. It is of the father, it is of the child, it is of society, which we wish to re-establish on its foundation, from which we believe it has perhaps swerved a little. (Page 575.)

Report of the New York Bureau of Labor Statistics, 1900.

The family furnishes the really fundamental education of the growing generation — the education of character; and the family life thus really determines the quality of the rising generation as efficient or non-efficient wealth producers. If a reduction in the hours of labor does promote the growth of a purer and better family life, it will unquestionably result in the production of greater material wealth on the part of the generation trained under its influence; nothing else in fact will so effectively diminish the vast number of criminals, paupers, and idlers, who, in the present generation, consume the people's substance. When one or both parents are away from home for twelve or thirteen hours (the necessary period for those who work ten hours) a day, the children receive comparatively little attention. What was said in the opening paragraph of this section in discussing the importance of a good family life in the training of character needs repeated emphasis, for it is the fundamental argument for a shorter working day. (Page 69.)

Hygiene of Occupations. Dr. Theodore Weyl. *Jena*, 1904.

Women bear the following generation whose health is essentially influenced by that of the mothers, and the State has a vital interest in securing for itself future generations capable of living and maintaining it. (Page 84.)

The Working Hours of Female Factory Hands. From reports of the Factory Inspectors collated by the Imperial Home Office. Berlin, 1905.

The reports from Marseburg, Erfurt, Breslau, Hanover, Wurtemberg, and Offenbach dwell upon the dependence of future generations — their total efficiency and value — upon the protection of working women and girls. (Page 111.)

President Roosevelt's Annual Message delivered to Second Session of 59th Congress. December 4, 1906.

More and more our people are growing to recognize the fact that the questions which are not merely of industrial but of social importance outweigh all others; and these two questions (labor of women and children) most emphatically come in the category of those which affect in the most far-reaching way the home life of the Nation.

Legislative Control of Women's Work. By S. P. Breckinridge. *Journal of Political Economy.* Vol. XIV. 1906.

The assumption of control over the conditions under which industrial women are employed is one of the most significant features of recent legislative policy. In many of the advanced industrial communities the State not only undertakes to prescribe a minimum of decency, safety, and healthfulness, below which its wage-earners may not be asked to go, but takes cognizance in several ways of sex differences and sex relationships. . . . In the third place, the State sometimes takes cognizance of the peculiarly close relationship which exists between the health of its women citizens and the physical vigor of future generations. . . . It has been declared a matter of public concern that no group of its women workers should be allowed to unfit themselves by excessive hours of work, by standing, or other physical strain, for the burden of mother-hood which each of them should be able to assume. (Page 107.)

The object of such control is the protection of the physical well-being of the community by setting a limit to the exploita-tion of the improvident, unworkmanlike, unorganized women who are yet the mothers, actual or prospective, of the coming genera-tion. (Pages 108, 109.)

Physical and Medical Aspects of Labor and Industry. By J. L. HOFFMAN. *Annals of Amer. Academy of Political and Social Science.* Vol. XXVII. May, 1906.

Again, in longevity, an increase of vitality, a decrease in disease liability, are all economic-elements of the greatest possible economic importance. They lie at the root of the true labor problem, for they determine in the long run the real and enduring progress, prosperity, and well-being of the masses. . . . It manifestly must be to the advantage of the State, and the employers of labor, that nothing within reason be left undone to raise to the highest possible standard the level of national physique and of health and indus-trial efficiency. . . . The interests of the nation, of wage-earners as a class, and of society as a whole, transcend the narrow and selfish interests of short-sighted employers of labor, who, disre-garding the teachings of medical and other sciences, manage in-dustry and permit the existence of conditions contrary to a sound industrial economy and a rational humanitarianism.

Labor Laws for Women in Germany. DR. ALICE SALOMON. *Pub-lished by the Women's Industrial Council. London,* 1907.

A study of the laws relating to female labor reveals that it has been the special aim of the legislators to protect and preserve the health of the women in their character as wives and as the mothers of future generations. On the one hand, the regulations are intended to pre-vent injury to health through over-long hours, or the resumption of work too soon after confinement, often the cause of serious illness which may render the patient incapable of bearing healthy offspring. . . . But if work in the factory be a necessity for women — even for married ones — it is all the more desirable that protective legislation should be so extended and worked out in such detail as to ensure the fullest attainment of its object, viz.: protection for the health of the female working population, as well as for the family and the home. (Page 5.)

Report of the Maine Bureau of Labor Statistics, 1892.

Employers should realize that long hours at a severe tension are a cause of irritation among their employees, and they become ripe for almost any trouble, and trifles are often sufficient to precipitate violent strikes. The real cause of many of these strikes is overwork. (Page 11.)

(2) THE EFFECT OF WOMEN'S OVERWORK ON FUTURE GENERATIONS

Report of the Massachusetts Bureau of Labor Statistics, 1871.

14. Progressive physical deterioration produced by family labor in factories. It is well known that like begets like, and if the parents are feeble in constitution, the children must also inevitably be feeble. Hence, among that class of people, you find many puny, sickly, partly developed children; every generation growing more and more so.

15. Connection between continuous factory labor and premature old age. It is a fact, patent to every one, that premature old age is fully developed, in consequence of long hours of labor and close confinement. Very few live to be old that work in a factory. (Page 504.)

Proceedings of the French Senate, July 9, 1891. Arguments for a Ten-hour Day for Women.

The woman wage-earner, gentlemen, does not always live at the mill-gates; she is therefore obliged to make a half or three-quarters' hour journey before she arrives; consequently she will leave home at half-past five in the morning, only to return at half-past eight or nine o'clock in the evening. Is that living? Under such circumstances can a woman truly care for her children and her home? (Page 581.)

Report of the Maryland Bureau of Industrial Statistics, 1896.

Once inside the walls of the factory a weary day's work of ten hours' duration is begun, with an intermission for lunch at noon. . . .

When the day's work is at last over, the wearied crowd trooping from their place of employment hasten in all directions to their homes, which in many instances are in the extreme suburbs of the city. Once home, they swallow a hasty supper and soon retire to a needed and deserved rest, with no pleasant anticipations for the morrow.

What lives are these for future wives and mothers? Future generations will answer. (Page 52.)

Report of the United States Industrial Commission, 1901.

Factory life brings incidentally new and depressing effects, which those whose experience has been wholly agricultural do not appreciate. But the experience of States which have pushed their way from agricultural to manufacturing industries, and have found that their delay in protecting their factory employees has weakened the physical and moral strength of the new generation of working people, would seem to be an experience which the citizens of new manufacturing States should hope to avoid. (Page 788.)

Report of the Committee on the Early Closing of Shops Bill, British House of Lords, 1901.

Sir W. MacCormac, President of the Royal College of Surgeons:

And you can hardly expect that women who have been suffering from such long hours should become the mothers of healthy children?

That is what I ventured to hint. It must have an influence on their offspring undoubtedly.

. . . It is gradual and progressive in its effect, and it goes on, I am afraid, in a cumulative degree.

You mean that from generation to generation the population will become feebler and feebler, and less able to resist disease?

It must suffer from the influence of it, no doubt. (Page 119.)

Report of the Wisconsin Bureau of Labor Statistics, 1903–1904.

In certain fields of industry, like the manufacture of cotton goods or hosiery and knit goods, we may find the establishments paying the lowest wages, working their employees the longest hours, and under the worst sanitary conditions, temporarily driving out of the field of competition those establishments paying the best wages, working their employees a reasonable length of time surrounded by the best sanitary conditions; but if the process is allowed to continue, the nation tolerating it will certainly revert to a state of discontent, poverty, and crime, which no agency or force can overcome so well as wise factory legislation strictly and judiciously enforced. (Page 137.)

Besides this many eminent students of social conditions maintain

that in countries where industries have been allowed to run for cen-
turies without any form of regulation, pauperism and crime are more
prevalent than in those countries where regulation exists. Also, in
countries where regulations have been imposed and withdrawn, misery
and want have risen and fallen in almost direct proportion to the
imposition and withdrawal of such regulation, and poor relief has
ebbed and flowed in almost the same proportion. (Page 140.)

*The Working Hours of Female Factory Hands. From Reports of the
Factory Inspectors, Collated by the Imperial Home Office. Berlin,
1905.*

The report for Würtemberg says, in regard to the injurious effect
of factory work: "The children of such mothers — according to the
unanimous testimony of nurses, physicians, and others who were
interrogated on this important subject — are mostly pale and weakly;
when these in turn, as usually happens, must enter upon factory work
immediately upon leaving school, to contribute to the support of the
family, it is impossible for a sound, sturdy, enduring race to develop."
(Page 113.)

The Case for the Factory Acts. Edited by Mrs. Sidney Webb.

The question arises, however, whether on philanthropic grounds
alone individuals of mature years can be denied the right to work as
long and as unhealthily as they like. The Acts of 1891 and 1895 show
signs of a recognition, if a tardy one, that the real grounds of interference with industry are considerations of public health and safety.
The old idea of protecting certain classes of workers because they are
not "free agents" is more and more felt to be irrelevant, if not mean-
ingless. There are still those who ask in astonishment, "May not
a man, may not a woman, employ their capital or their labor as they
choose?" But the State says, with a less and less hesitating sound,
"Not under conditions wasteful of the life, or destructive of the efficiency, of those employed, or dangerous to the safety and well-being
of the community." To this conclusion it has been driven by inquiry
into the conditions of public health. (Page 122.)

The Case for the Factory Acts. Edited by Mrs. Sidney Webb.

It may be enough for the individual employer if his workpeople
remain alive during the period for which he hires them. But for the

continued efficiency of the nation's industry, it is indispensable that its citizens should not merely continue to exist for a few months or years, but should be well brought up as children, and maintained for their full normal life unimpaired in health, strength, and character. The human beings of a community form as truly a portion of its working capital as its land, its machinery, or its cattle. If the employers in a particular trade are able to take such advantage of the necessities of their workpeople as to hire them for wages actually insufficient to provide enough food, clothing, and shelter to maintain them and their children in health; if they are able to work them for hours so long as to deprive them of adequate rest and recreation; or if they subject them to conditions so dangerous or insanitary as positively to shorten their lives, that trade is clearly using up and destroying a part of the nation's working capital.

. . . Industries yielding only a bare minimum of momentary subsistence are therefore not really self-supporting. In deteriorating the physique, intelligence, and character of their operatives, they are drawing on the capital stock of the nation. And even if the using up is not actually so rapid as to prevent the "sweated" workers from producing a new generation to replace them, the trade is none the less parasitic. In persistently deteriorating the stock it employs, it is subtly draining away the vital energy of the community. It is taking from these workers, week by week, more than its wages can restore to them. A whole community might conceivably thus become parasitic on itself, or, rather, upon its future. (Page 20.)

History of Factory Legislation. HUTCHINS *and* HARRISON.

So far from being regarded as romantically philanthropic, like the ten-hour bill of 1844 . . . the bills of 1867 were taken as a matter of common sense and economic prudence. . . . Only a certain amount of work is to be got out of women and children in the twenty-four hours. . . . Nothing can be gained in the end by anticipating our resources, and to employ women and children unduly is simply to run in debt to Nature. (Page 167.)

Infant Mortality. A Social Problem. GEORGE NEWMAN, M. D. London, 1906.

A nation grows out of its children, and if its children die in infancy, it means that the sources of a nation's population are being sapped, and further that the conditions that kill such a large proportion of infants injure many of those which survive. Last year, 1905, there was a loss to the nation of 120,000 dead infants, in England and Wales alone, a figure which is almost exactly one quarter of all the deaths in England and Wales in that year. (Page 2.)

And this enormous sacrifice of human life is being repeated year by year and is not growing less. (Page 7.)

Nor is England alone. . . . The birth rate is declining in civilized nations with few exceptions; and the same may be said of the death rate. But the infant mortality rate, as a rule, is stationary or even increasing.

There are two features, however, which appear to be common to the high infant mortality districts, namely, a high density of population and a considerable degree of manufacturing industry. (Page 26.)

II. SHORTER HOURS THE ONLY POSSIBLE PROTECTION

This needed protection to women can be afforded only through shortening the hours of labor. A decrease of the intensity of exertion is not feasible.

Report of the United States Industrial Commission, 1901

It is certain that any programme for reducing this intensity of exertion must fail. The entire tendency of industry is in the direction of an increased exertion. Any restrictions on output must work to the disadvantage of American industry, and the employers are often right in their demand, usually successful, that such restrictions be abandoned. This being true, there is but one alternative if the working population is to be protected in its health and trade longevity, namely, a reduction of the hours of labor. (Page 763.)

Industrial Conference . . . of the National Civic Federation. New York, 1902.

The factory system makes this (shortening hours) more and more necessary in proportion as it is perfected in its mechanism. It becomes all the time more and more exacting. The greater the perfection of the machinery or the method, the more attention is required. . . . (Page 173.)

And whatever is necessary to make the most of the machinery is important to the successful conduct of the industry. If that makes the laborers tired, then, so far as the employer is concerned, they must be tired; if it calls for too much strenuous attention, too much nerve exhaustion, then the nerve exhaustion must come or the machinery is a failure. The remedy for this cannot be found in slackening up on the demands for economic output and effectiveness in the machinery. . . . The remedy for that must come on the other side, shortening the day, not slackening the effort. The tension may not be lessened, but the hours may be reduced. The exhaustion on the laborer must be avoided, but it cannot be avoided by reducing production . . . they (employers) find that modern business is more exacting than ever and . . . that to slacken is to fail. Consequently they find that long vacations are necessary to avoid physical exhaustion. But long vacations are impossible for laborers . . . they must have relief by lessening the duration of the pressure every day. (Page 174.)

III. THE GENERAL BENEFITS OF SHORT HOURS

History, which has illustrated the deterioration due to long hours, bears witness no less clearly to the regeneration due to the shorter working day. To the individual and to society alike, shorter hours have been a benefit wherever introduced. The married and unmarried working woman is enabled to obtain the decencies of life outside of working hours. With the improvement in home life, the tone of the entire community is raised. Wherever sufficient time has elapsed since the establishment of the shorter working day, the succeeding generation has shown extraordinary improvement in physique and morals.

A. *Good Effect on the Individual Health, Home Life, etc.*

Report of the Massachusetts Bureau of Labor Statistics, 1871.

Their hours of labor should not exceed ten hours per day, for, as we have seen, 85 + per cent of the working girls of Boston do their own housework and sewing either wholly or in part, and this homework must be done in addition to that performed for their employers. (Page 558.)

Report of the British Chief Inspector of Factories and Workshops, 1877.

Ten years ago, when I made the first effort to introduce the Factory Acts in London, I was frequently met with the statement on the part of employers that the tendency of the Act would be to encourage prostitution, because by giving the women an enforced leisure they would be exposed to additional temptation. I was loath to believe any such theory, and I am glad to say that, so far as my experience during the last ten years goes, the fears thus expressed have never been realized. There has been quite a revolution during that period in the conditions on which seamstress work is carried on in the metropolis. The employment of them in workshops and fac-

tories has increased enormously, but I can find no employer willing
to commit himself to the opinion that in their respective classes
there has been any deterioration in the character and the conduct of
the workpeople. All the evidence indeed which I have obtained
goes to establish the contrary. (Page 14.)

Report of the New York Bureau of Labor Statistics, 1900.

The wife's life is darkened even more by the long-hour day, especially if she also be a working woman. Even if the day be one of
only ten hours, she must arise as early as five o'clock to prepare
breakfast for her husband and herself, so that they may be at their
work places at seven. Beginning at that early hour her day will be
a very long one. (Page 69.)

*The Working Hours of Female Factory Hands. From reports of the
Factory Inspectors collated by the Imperial Home Office. Berlin, 1905.*

The inspector for Upper Bavaria dwells upon the advantage ac-
cruing to the health of working-girls as follows:
"In the matter of health the shortening of the working hours is of
unusual value, because for them free time is not resting time, as it is
for a man. For the working-girl on her return from the factory there
is a variety of work waiting. She has her room to keep clean and in
order, her laundry work to do, clothes to repair and clean, and, besides
this, she should be learning to keep house if her future household is
not to be disorderly and a failure." (Page 111.)

Many inspectors urge the need of shortening the hours of labor
on grounds of morality. From Offenbach it is reported: "The
period before marriage is the time for learning the future profession,
but during this period the factory worker is exposed to strain and
fatigue, which hinder her bodily development and deprive her of
educational opportunity. Desirable, therefore, would be a reduction
of the working hours which should give to married women more time
for their housework and family life, and to the younger unmarried
women the opportunity to learn the art of home-making, because
upon this the health, welfare, and prosperity of her whole family
will depend." (Page 113.)

B. *Good Effect on the General Welfare*

Report of the British Chief Inspector of Factories and Workshops,
1859.

I think I can show that the Factory Acts have put an end to the premature decrepitude of the former long-hour workers; that they have enlarged their social and intellectual privileges; that by making them masters of their own time they have given them a moral energy which is directing them to the eventual possession of political power; and that they have lifted them up high in the scale of rational beings, compared with that which they had attained in 1833. Moreover, I think I can further prove that all this has been accomplished without any prejudice whatever to our commercial prosperity. . . .

There is no need to raise again to public view the crooked and attenuated creatures of that bygone period. . . . The "factory leg" and the "curved spine" were a proverb and a reproach. . . .

How happily then may we turn to the contemplation of it in 1859! The proverb has died a natural death, and the reproach is all but taken away. There is scarcely now to be seen in any of the manufacturing districts a crooked leg or a distorted spine as the result of factory labor. . .

The physical condition of the future mothers of the working classes may be challenged to meet that of any mothers of any country. (Page 47.)

Report of the Massachusetts Bureau of Statistics of Labor, 1873.
On Results of Ten-hour Labor Law in England.

Lord Ashley said: " Upon the good moral and social influence of the change, the testimony is most favorable from the clergymen and school teachers throughout Yorkshire and Lancaster. How have the women used their time? Hundreds of them are attending evening school, — learning to read and write and to knit and sew, things that they could not have learned under the twelve-hour system.

" A burial society testifies to the diminution of burial although the cholera was upon the town, and that the diminution was among children under five years of age, and he assumes as a reason that mothers can get home earlier and give that attention to children which no hired nurse can ensure.

" The Catholic priests at Stockport and Bolton testify that the number of factory workers attending schools has more than doubled, and that there was not the slightest doubt that the moral, social, and physical condition of the people had improved." (Page 491.)

Report of the New Jersey Bureau of Statistics of Labor and Industry, 1886.

The Factory Acts were believed to be the death-blow to English manufactures, and they have made labor more efficient, more intelligent, more decent, and more continuous without trenching on profits.

In 1851 and 1852 those who advocated that ten hours should be a legal day's work were denounced as demagogues, and the ten-hour plan as a humbug which could only tend to reduce the wages proportionately, while all kinds of evil results were sure to follow its application, especially to agricultural labor. But we have seen ten hours become the rule; wages have not fallen, and many of those who prophesied disaster are now as loud in their praises of its beneficence as the friends of the change. (Page 231.)

Report of the Massachusetts Chief of the District Police, 1889.

The good results of shortening the hours of labor were soon apparent, in the substantial disappearance of discontent among those affected thereby; in the maintenance of the standard of factory productions, both as to quantity and quality; and in placing Massachusetts in the lead, where, by her history and her aspirations, she rightfully belonged.

. . . If experience has shown anything in this matter, it has been the wisdom and statesmanship of the body of laws in our Public Statutes and additions thereto, which are known as industrial legislation. It is sixteen years since the ten-hour law was enacted; and it is entirely safe to say that, if it were stricken from the statutes to-day, not an influential voice would be raised within our borders in favor of the restoration of the order of things which that law changed. The increase of public interest in matters of this kind is a very significant fact. (Page 7.)

Report of the Illinois Chief Inspector of Factories, 1895.

In England the principle of the regulation of the hours of work of women and children has been established for more than a generation; and the regeneration of the working class in that country, from the degradation in which it was sunk in 1844, is attributed to the Factory Acts, and especially to this essential feature of them. (Page 5.)

French Review of Hygiene and Sanitary Police. Vol. XVIII. 1896.

All the world knows well that there is much to do, and that, if our legislation has already bettered conditions, new ameliorations are desirable, but they will come, I think, only through the pressure of public opinion, . . . which will become exacting . . . when doctors have made clear the utility of a protection which regards not only the woman, but, secondarily, the child to be born by her; when it knows better that to protect the mother is an absolute necessity for the future of the race. (Page 193.)

Report of the New York Bureau of Labor Statistics, 1900.

But the good accomplished by each successive factory law was so clearly apparent, that even capitalistic Parliament could not refuse to continue the policy of labor protection. The evidence that this policy wrought a revolutionary change in the amount of crime, pauperism, and misery is superabundant; but it is too familiar to warrant repetition now. (Page 49).

The best evidence of the overwhelming success of the short-hour law from all points of view is afforded by the complete conversion of its opponents. Thus it came to pass that in 1860, when a bill was introduced to extend the ten-hour law to other branches of the textile industry, J. A. Roebuck, who had originally opposed with bitterness this kind of legislation, made the following recantation:

" I am about to speak on this question under somewhat peculiar circumstances. Very early in my parliamentary career Lord Ashley, now the Earl of Shaftesbury, introduced a bill of this description. I, being an ardent political economist, as I am now, opposed the measure, . . . and was very much influenced in my opposition by what the gentlemen of Lancashire said. They declared that it was the last half-hour of the work performed by their operatives which made all their profits, and that if we took away that last half-hour we should ruin the manufacturers of England. I listened to that statement and trembled for the manufacturers of England [a laugh]; but Lord Ashley persevered. Parliament passed the bill which he brought in. From that time down to the present the factories of this country have been under State control, and I appeal to this House whether the manufacturers of England have suffered by this legislation."

Sir James Graham, another persistent antagonist of the short-hour laws, followed Mr. Roebuck with a similar recantation:

" I am sorry once more to be involved in a short-time discussion. I have, however, a confession to make to the House. . . . Experience has shown to my satisfaction that many of the predictions formerly made against the factory bill have not been verified by the result, as, on the whole, that great measure of relief for women and children has contributed to the well-being and comfort of the working classes, while it has not injured their masters. The enactment of the present bill ought to approach as nearly as possible the Factory Act. . . . By the vote I shall give to-night, I will endeavor to make some amends for the course I pursued in earlier life in opposing the factory bill." (Page 51.)

All travellers unite in testifying to the wonderful energy displayed in their work by the wage-earners of Australia. Such energy is a product not so much of the stimulating climate as the high standard of comfort made possible by the short working-day. Considerable evidence might be adduced in support of the following enthusiastic opinion of John Rae (" Eight Hours for Work," page 312).

The more we examine the subject the more irresistibly is the impression borne in from all sides that there is growing up in Australia, and very largely in consequence of the eight-hour day, a working class, who, for general morale, intelligence, and industrial efficiency is probably already superior to that of any other branch of our Anglo-Saxon race, and for happiness, cheerfulness, and all-around comfort of life has never had its equal in the world before. (Page 59.)

Report of the United States Industrial Commission, 1901.

Lessening of hours leaves more opportunity and more vigor for the betterment of character, the improvement of the home. . . . For these reasons the short work-day for working people brings an advantage to the entire community. (Page 773.)

Night-work of Women in Industry. PROF. ETIENNE BAUER. *Jena*, 1903.

Above all, there is perceptible in all the countries in which women are protected, a reduction in the mortality both of women and of children.

For England the convincing argument on this point has often been produced. There, since the establishment of the normal working day the mortality figures for working-women have fallen much lower than those for men. This proportion was as follows: 1841–1850, 23.11 per cent for men, 21.58 per cent for women. From 1881–1890, 20.22 per cent for men, 18.01 per cent for women.

The diminution in the two figures taken together is to be attributed to the great advance in hygiene achieved in the interval, and the relatively greater decrease in the mortality of women is to be attributed to the protective legislation. (Page 37.)

Report of the Wisconsin Bureau of Labor Statistics, 1903–1904.

No private individual has any more moral right to exhaust the working energy and working capital of a nation without giving "value received" than he has to take the life of an employee outright. The only difference is that one is a slower criminal process than the other. It is not enough that workmen should obtain barely enough for their labor to enable them to live, but they should receive a competency. They should receive as much energy from their employers in food, clothing, homes, and furnishings amid healthful surroundings as they give to their employers in the articles they produce.

The stronger, healthier, and more intelligent a laborer is, the more wealth he represents. The laborers of a nation represent its working capital just as the hands of the farmer, his horse, or his ox represent his working capital. And the stronger and healthier either may be, the more capital it represents. The more efficient this capital becomes, the more wealth will be produced. Machinery operators represent the working capital of the manufacturer, and he owes it to the nation which protects him in his business to do everything in his power to increase this working capital and keep it in the highest possible state of efficiency. (Page 129.)

The regulation of factories either by law or by special agreement worked marvellous changes in England. In the course of half a century the "sweated" laborers of this great country whose course of life seemed almost run became energetic, self-reliant, intelligent, and efficient workers, owning their own homes, amid wholesome surroundings, and working a reasonable number of hours for a day's work.

Not only is factory legislation sound in principle, but wherever put to the test it has been found sound in practice as well. (Page 137.)

History of Factory Legislation. Hutchins *and* Harrison.

In 1861 the president of the Economic Section of the British Association could say in his address that the results of that bill (ten-hours bill) were "something of which all parties might well be proud. There is in truth a general assent that if there has been one change which more than another has strengthened and consolidated the social fabric in this part of the island, has cleared away a mass of depravity and discontent, has placed the manufacturing enterprise of the country on a safe basis, and has conferred upon us resources against the effects of foreign competition which can scarcely be overvalued, it is precisely the changes which have been brought about by the sagacious and persevering and successful efforts to establish in manufacturing occupations a sound system of legal interference with the hours of labor." (Page 122.)

The Case for the Factory Acts. Edited by Mrs. Sidney Webb.

The two great industries which, at the beginning of the nineteenth century, were conspicuous for the worst horrors of sweating were the textile manufactures and coal-mining. Between 1830 and 1850 the parliamentary inquiries into these trades disclosed sickening details of starvation wages, incredibly long hours, and conditions of work degrading to decency and health. The remedy applied was the substitution, for individual bargaining between employer and operative, of a compulsory minimum set forth in common rules prescribing standard conditions of employment.

. . . What was the result? Fortunately, there is no dispute. Every one who knows these great industries agrees in declaring that the horrors which used to prevail under individual bargaining have been brought to an end. The terms "cotton-operative" and "coal-miner," instead of denoting typically degraded workers, as they did in 1830, are now used to designate the very aristocracy of our labor. And when, to-day, those who are interested in the industrial progress of women need an example of a free and self-reliant class of female wage-earners, earning full subsistence, enjoying adequate leisure, and capable of effective organization, they are compelled to turn to the great body of Lancashire cotton-weavers, now for half a century "restricted" in every feature of their contract. (Page 36.)

IV. ECONOMIC ASPECT OF SHORT HOURS

A. *Effect on Output*

The universal testimony of manufacturing countries tends to prove that the regulation of the working day acts favorably upon output. With long hours, output declines; with short hours, it rises. The heightened efficiency of the workers, due to the shorter day, more than balances any loss of time. Production is not only increased, but improved in quality.

(1) SHORTER HOURS INCREASE EFFICIENCY, AND THUS PREVENT REDUCTION OF OUTPUT

Report of the United States Industrial Commission, 1900.

Those States which are just now advancing to the position of manufacturing communities might well learn from these examples the lesson that permanent industrial progress cannot be built upon the physical exhaustion of women and children. . . . A reduction in hours has never lessened the working-people's ability to compete in the markets of the world. States with shorter work-days actually manufacture their products at a lower cost than States with longer workdays. (Page 788.)

History of Factory Legislation. HUTCHINS *and* HARRISON.

Bleachers in a petition to their employers, 1853: We believe the result generally is such as to corroborate our statement that short hours produce more work and that of a better quality than under the old system. (Page 132.)

Massachusetts Bureau of Statistics of Labor. **1872.**

The testimony of those who have adopted the shorter time is almost unanimous in its favor. Many reported an improved condition of the employees. No instance is given of decreased wages, though many report an increase, not only in wages, but in production. All of the arguments against reduction made by those working eleven hours and over are answered by those who have adopted the shorter time, and worked under that system for years. The advocates of eleven hours have utterly failed to sustain themselves in their continued adhesion to a system that England outgrew twenty-two years ago; a system unworthy of our State and nation, and one that would not last a month if the victims of it were men instead of women and children, as most of them are. (Page 240.)

Massachusetts Bureau of Statistics of Labor. **1873.**

The overseer (of Pemberton Mills, Lawrence) informed us that they took the result of every half-hour's work, and upon inquiring the relative product of the different hours, he assured us that invariably the last hour was the least productive. (Page 246.)

Hon. William Gray, Treasurer of the Atlantic Mills, Lawrence, began the ten-hour experiment with the operatives in his employ, June, 1867, and his testimony concerning its practical and financial success may be regarded as nearly, if not quite, authoritative and decisive. Ten and three-fourths hours had been the running time of this mill previous to this date. The result of this reduction is substantially as follows:

In three and a half years from the time of the change, the product of the hours was fully equal to the product of ten and three-fourths hours, and this was accomplished with old machinery that had been running for twenty years with very little change.

With no material change in machinery, these results appear.

First. An improvement in the operatives directly after adopting ten hours, — which improvement has been going on; and they now have the best set of workers that have been in the mills for fifteen years, this being the opinion of the agent and overseers, as well as the treasurer. (Page 495.)

Factory and Workshops Act Commission, 1875. *British Sessional Papers,* 1876. Vol. XXX.

Testimony of Phillip Grant, representing operatives:

During the agitation for the ten-hours bill in the year 1844 or 1845, he (a cotton-spinner at Preston) reduced his time voluntarily to eleven hours instead of twelve, and at the end of twelve months he reported, as Mr. Hugh Mason did, that he had got a better quality of work and more of it in the eleven hours than he had in the twelve, and that is obvious to anybody who understands the process of following a machine. (Paragraph 8582.)

Report of the British Factory Inspector, 1877.

The women at the close of the twelve hours, which period constitutes the usual day's work, were tired and exhausted, and hardly did enough after that to pay for the gas consumed. Book sewers and folders are all paid by piecework, and if overtime were continued for a few weeks together their earnings would soon fall to about the same amount as when they worked the regular hours.

Report of Massachusetts Bureau of Statistics of Labor, 1881.

It is apparent that Massachusetts with ten hours produces as much per man or per loom or per spindle, equal grades being considered, as other States with eleven and more hours; and also that wages here rule as high, if not higher, than in the States where the mills run longer time. (Page 457.)

But perhaps the most emphatic testimony is that of another carpet mill employing about twelve hundred persons. This mill, which has been running but ten hours for several years, and has during this period tried the experiment of running overtime, gives the following results. The manager said, "I believe, with proper management and supervision, the same help will produce as many goods, and of superior quality, in ten hours as they will in eleven. I judge so from the fact that during certain seasons, being pushed for goods, we have run up to nine o'clock, and for the first month the production was increased materially. After this, however, the help would grow listless, and the production would fall off and the quality of the goods deteriorate." (Page 460.)

The reason is, the flesh and blood of the operatives have only so much work in them, and it was all got out in ten hours, and no more could be got out in twelve; and what was got extra in the first month was taken right out of the life of the operatives. (Page 461.)

Report of the Connecticut Bureau of Labor Statistics, 1886.

Down to a certain point, the nations who work shorter hours not merely do better work, but more work than their competitors. In Russia the hands work twelve hours a day; in Germany and France, eleven; in England, nine. Yet nine hours a day of English work mean more than twelve hours of Russian work.

The laborer receives better wages, and at the same time the manufacturer gets a larger product — so much larger that it is the Russian, the German, or the Frenchman who requires protection against his English competitor in spite of the longer hours and lower day's wages. (Page 16.)

Report of the German Imperial Factory Inspectors, 1886–1887.

Report for Mittel and Unter Franken:
It has been repeatedly shown that a shortening of the working day does not lessen the value of the work done, because owing to the effort to prevent a decrease in the income, the shorter time is more profitably used. (Page 86.)

Belgium. Commission du Travail, 1886. Report of the Sessions of Inquiry into Industrial Labor. Brussels, 1887.

But it is shown that everything which makes the worker more strong, more healthy, more energetic, more intelligent, etc. (and these will be the results of greater leisure, and the observance of rules prescribed for hygiene, upon the subject of the hours of labor and rest), make him also more productive. Therefore the introduction of reforms indicates strongly that the final result will be a very great increase of production with a shorter time period for work. (Page 65.)

International Conference in Relation to Labor Legislation. Berlin, 1890.

Alone, the nations hesitate to reduce the hours of work for fear of competition, although, with modern machinery, experience has abundantly proved that the countries with the shortest working day attain the maximum of production. These are the countries that produce under good conditions most cheaply; that are most prosperous, and most feared as competitors in the world's markets. (Page 88.)

Report of the Maine Bureau of Labor Statistics, 1890.

In my State, since the adoption of the ten hours in lieu of the eleven hours in mills and factories where machinery is employed, it is the universal verdict of manufacturers that their product is as great under the ten-hour system as it was under the eleven-hour system, and I think that the same answer comes from every State that has adopted the ten-hour system.

Conditions of Female Labor in Toronto, by JEAN THOMSON SCOTT. *Toronto, 1891.*

Experts say that the cost of production in the cotton trade is actually the lowest where the wages are the highest and the hours shortest. Dr. Schulze Gaevernitz shows this specifically, because the standard of living of the workers has been raised and with it their general intelligence, enabling them to do more in a shorter time — what I have called "intensive work."

. . . That is the opinion of experts on the trade throughout the world. They say that all over the world the cost of production is lowest where wages are highest and hours shortest. (Page 44.)

Report of the German Imperial Factory Inspectors, 1893.

In most establishments the working day was eleven hours, not seldom the ten-hour day was introduced. The shorter day turned out well in all cases. (Liegnitz.)

In a cigar-box and wrapper-mold factory all adult workers were given uniform working hours in summer and winter, — a nine-hour day, from seven to six, with two hours free time at noon. The owner asserts that in this shorter time no less work is done than formerly in the longer time, the eleven-hours day. (Kassel.) (Page 155.)

Report of the Imperial German Factory Inspectors, 1893.

The week workers expressed anxiety in many cases lest their wage be cut after the new regulations took effect, but our observation is that, in most cases, the pay of the women wage-earners remained unchanged. (Page 155.)

Report of the Connecticut Bureau of Labor Statistics, 1893.

As to the effect of reducing the working time to nine hours daily, no inquiry was made, but several employers stated voluntarily to agents of the bureau that their experience proved to them that production was as large in nine hours as it had been in ten. (Page 28.)

Report of the German Imperial Factory Inspectors, 1895.

The report of amount and value of the work done in the reduced working day are also of interest. The fact that the value of the work is not in proportion to the hours of work is but slowly understood. A wool factory reduced their working day by one hour, in accordance with the law of June 1, 1891; subtracting the rest periods, it now amounts to ten and one-half hours. The owners assert that the amount and value of work done by both males and females remain the same, while calls upon sick fund have greatly diminished. (Page 370.)

Report of the German Imperial Factory Inspectors, 1898.

In one laundry in Plauen, where the hours of the workers have been reduced from eleven to ten hours, it has been proved that the women accomplish fully as much as before this reduction. In a jute spinning and weaving factory in Cassel the ten-hour day was provisionally introduced at the request of the hands in September. Thus far it has worked so well that the shorter day will probably be retained. (Page 106.)

Report of New York Bureau of Labor Statistics, 1900.

Fortunately, statistics are at hand which afford simple but fairly effective tests of the assertion that Massachusetts industries are threatened with ruin by restrictive labor legislation. In the first place, Massachusetts' cotton industry, the business chiefly affected by short-hour laws, has fully kept pace with that of rival States in the North.

Certain facts appear with distinctness, one of which is that the cotton industry of Massachusetts has not only grown steadily throughout the period of short-hour legislation, but — what is far more impressive — has made larger gains than are shown by the adjacent States with less radical short-hour laws. In 1870, four years before the enactment of the ten-hour law, Massachusetts had 39.5 per cent of all the cotton spindles in the North Atlantic States; six years after the passage of that law Massachusetts' proportion was 45 per cent;

in 1890 it was 47.5 per cent, and in 1900 53.5 per cent. It is difficult to see what clearer proof could be demanded of the beneficial results of the Massachusetts short-hour laws of 1874 (sixty hours a week) and 1892 (fifty-eight hours). (Page 55.)

In all those departments of the factory in which wages are paid by piece-work — and these constitute probably not less than four-fifths of the whole, the proportion to fixed daily wages being daily on the increase — it has been found that the quantity produced in ten and one-half hours falls little short of that formerly obtained from twelve hours. In some cases it is said to be equal. This is accounted for partly by the increased stimulus given to ingenuity to make the machines more perfect and capable of increased speed, but it arises far more from the workpeople by improved health, by absence of that weariness and exhaustion which the long hours occasioned, and by their increased cheerfulness and activity, being enabled to work more steadily and diligently and to economize time, intervals of rest while at their work being now less necessary. (Page 50.)

Report of the United States Industrial Commission, 1900. Vol. VII.

It is also claimed that a shorter day would not lessen production even in hand work. Perhaps you would be interested in the experiment of a gentleman who had an establishment in Fitchburg where were made the balls used in bicycle bearings. When he first took charge of the establishment they were running ten hours a day, with the exception of Saturday, when they ran eight, making fifty-eight hours a week. Women were employed in inspecting the balls. They do this by touch, which becomes very perfect in time and sensitive to the least imperfection; the balls are dropped into boxes, the perfect balls into one box and the imperfect ones into others, graded according to the imperfection. In the afternoon the work done by one woman in the morning is inspected by another, and thus there is a double inspection. He became persuaded that there was a certain strain in this work on the eyes, the fingers, and the attention, and finally he made up his mind that shorter hours would be better for the women and would not lessen the amount of work done — it would be better for their health and quite as well for the business. Accordingly he directed the women's department to be run but nine hours a day. At first the women were very much distressed. As they were paid by the number of thousands of balls inspected, they thought it would permit them to earn less money; but they soon found that they did just as many balls in the nine hours as they had heretofore done

in the ten; and they had besides ten minutes' vacation in the middle
of the morning session and in the afternoon. Later, the time was
shortened to eight hours and a half. There was not so much objection
as at first, because they began to see what the object was, and they
soon found they did just as much in eight and a half as in nine. At
last accounts the time had been shortened to eight hours, and it was
believed it could be cut down to seven and one-half. (Page 63.)

Report of the United States Industrial Commission, 1900.

What I wanted to show was that the trend of intelligent business
management is to the conclusion that when a person who is doing the
work has less strain upon him, he will get out more work up to a certain limit, in less time; and where the work is done by the piece it is
done with less dawdling and more diligence, nor is it so hard to work
with that severe attention for less time as it is to work longer hours
with less attention. (Page 64.)

Report of the New York Department of Factory Inspection, 1901.

It was feared by employers that to reduce the hours of labor
was to reduce the quantity of products, and that in the competition for markets the longer hours would have a decided advantage
over the shorter hours; but it has been demonstrated that the
lessening of the hours of labor does not, within certain limits,
result in a decrease, but rather in an increase of products instead.

Another phase of the subject has also come to the front gradually in the course of this agitation for a shorter work-day. It is
that quality of product may be improved by a shorter day, and
by this improvement in quality of the product has come to be considered the improvement of the quality of the laborer himself.
(Page 562.)

Factory People and their Employers. By E. L. SHUEY. *New
York, 1900.*

Among the most desirable things is the matter of shorter hours
for women. The experience of a number of leading manufacturers
has indicated that equal results may be obtained in many forms of
manufacture in the shorter hours. Fels & Co. of Philadelphia
gradually reduced the time of their women from ten to eight hours,
girls working five days in the week. At the same time wages have
been practically increased. The Levy Bros. Co. (England) has

had a similar experience. The National Cash Register Co. in the same manner reduced its hours for women from ten to eight. (Page 113.)

Report of the New York Bureau of Labor, 1901.

Prof. F. A. Walker thus sums up this general conclusion: " It is the general belief of intelligent and disinterested men that every successive reduction of the hours of labor from fifteen hours to the limit, say ten or eleven hours in ordinary mercantile pursuits, effected not a proportional loss of product, not a loss at all, but a positive gain, especially if not only the present productive power of the body of laborers is considered, but also the keeping up of the full supply of labor in full numbers and unimpaired strength from generation to generation." (Page 562.)

The Case for the Factory Acts. Edited by Mrs. Sidney Webb. *London,* 1901.

The direct and constant result of enforcing standard conditions of employment is, . . . to raise the capacity of the workers. The prevention of excessive or irregular hours of work, the require-ment of healthy conditions, and the insistence on decency in the factory or workshop — the direct results of factory legislation — represent exactly what is required to extricate the mass of work-ing women from the slough of inefficiency in which they are unfortunately sunk. Hence, so far from regulation being any detriment to the persons regulated, it is, as all experience proves, a positive good. (Page 209.)

Report of the British Association for the Advancement of Science, 1902.

There was a general consensus of opinion that shorter hours and better sanitation enforced by legislation had been amongst the causes tending to increase the efficiency of women workers. (Page 287.)

Travail de Nuit des Femmes dans l'Industrie. Prof. Etienne Bauer. *Jena,* 1903.

Before the enactment of the German Imperial Law of 1891 restricting the hours of labor of women there, overtime work was already, in the industries concerned, occasional and irregular. The very great majority of the establishments affected were working regularly eleven hours a day or less as early as 1892.

Not one fact indicates that industry suffered under the restriction. The output, which, in a few establishments, diminished at first, soon regained its normal dimensions, thanks to the greater energy evinced by the employees. (Page 12.)

Bulletin of the French Labor Office, 1903.

There are establishments in which it may be affirmed, according to the statement of a district inspector of Nantes, that the production per hour increases as the number of hours per day decreases. These are the industries in which the personal qualities of the worker are an important factor in production. (Page 807.)

Report of the Wisconsin Bureau of Labor Statistics, 1903–1904.

Manufacturers maintain that by enforcing shorter hours they are unable to compete with those factories which are not hampered in this way. In order to test the truth or falsity of this claim, the Salford Iron Works of Manchester, England, voluntarily reduced the number of hours required for a day's work to eight. After giving the system a fair trial, the management declared that the character of work performed and wages paid remained about the same; that although a depression in trade took place about the same time this experiment was being made, and competition was exceedingly fierce, the output was greater and the receipts larger than under the old system. The Salford Iron Works continue the eight-hour system to the present day, and other allied industries and the arsenal works and dock-yards are following example. (Page 140.)

The Relation of Labor to the Law of To-day. By Lujo Brentano. *New York.*

Why then does an increase in wages and a decrease in the time of work in general lead to a greater capability for work? Because higher wages and a shorter day's work make it possible for laborers to increase and satisfy their physical and spiritual needs; because better food, more careful fostering, greater and more moral recreation increase the power to work, and because they increase the pleasure in labor. . . . In other words, an increase in wages and a decrease in the time of work lead to a greater performance, because they elevate the standard of living of the laborer, a higher standard of living necessarily spurs to greater intensity of labor, and at the same time makes the same possible. (Pages 233, 234.)

Getting a Living. By G. L. BOLEN.

Repeated shortening of the factory day has come because it was found that strength was saved, intelligence promoted, and that product and wages were both increased. (Pages 423, 424.)

(2) LONG HOURS RESULT IN INFERIOR QUALITY OF PRODUCT

Report of the Massachusetts Bureau of Labor Statistics, 1871.

The operatives vary in perfectness and productiveness as the day progresses; and if there should be a reduction to ten hours there would not be a loss of one-eleventh of the product. . . . I think it will be found that much of the cloth made during the eleventh hour is of poorer quality than the rest, and that the necessity of looking it over the next day and fixing it all right lessens the product of that next day. . . . I certainly believe that the productive capacity of a set of work-people may be lessened by increasing the hours of their daily work. The question is not legitimately one of arithmetic, nor can it be settled by argument about one-eleventh less or one-tenth more. It is a question to be settled by actual results on long-continued trial. (Page 498 ff.)

Report of the British Chief Inspector of Factories and Workshops, 1893.

Arguments against overtime (*i. e.*, two hours more than the daily ten and one-half):

1. That the work done during overtime is not equal, in amount or quality, to that done during the regular time.

Dangerous Trades. THOMAS OLIVER, M. D. *London,* 1902.

It is admitted that in iron-works and factories, where the hours of labor have been unusually long, say ten and eleven hours, the work done in the latter part of the day is not so good as that done in the forenoon.

Women in the Printing Trades. Edited by J. R. MacDonald. *London*, 1904.

From this it is evident that protection is viewed favorably by many employers, on the specific ground that it prevents systematic overtime. On the whole they are of the opinion that after overtime the next day's work suffers. (Page 82.)

B. used to work from 8 A. M. to 8 P. M. regularly, including Saturdays. . . . She disliked overtime, was tired out at the end of a day's work, and thought the other women were too, and she had often noticed how badly the work was done after eight or nine hours at it. Later on, as a forewoman, she noticed that the girls after overtime always loafed about the next day and did not work well. (Page 84.)

Another forewoman gave it as her deliberate opinion that when overtime is worked the piece workers do not make more, as a rule, for they get so tired that if they stay late one night, they work less the next day.

This is the unanimous view held by the forewomen, and it comes with considerable force from them, as it is they who have to arrange to get work done somehow within a certain time. They are the people who have to put on the pressure, and are in such a position as to see how any particular system of getting work done. (Page 87.)

Hours and Wages in Relation to Production. Luigi Brentano.

By degrees the employers themselves admitted that the last two hours, formerly considered indispensable, used generally to produce work far inferior to that of the preceding hours, and that owing to the greater industry of the employees, who no longer idled through the first hours of the day, the regular unbroken labor of the new working day was much more advantageous to the employees than the longer working day, with its alternations of overwork and indolence. So it came about, as a result of the curtailment of the working day, production did not diminish, but actually increased. (Page 29.)

In the report of the Stuttgart Chamber of Commerce of 1890 we find, on page 47, a corset factory reports: " Five years ago we returned to a ten-hour working day (with a half-hour pause in the morning and another in the afternoon) we find that our work-women can get through very much more with regular work for ten or even nine hours, than when the working day is longer." (Page 36.)

B. *Effect on Regularity of Employment*

Wherever the employment of women has been pro-hibited for more than ten hours in one day, a more equal distribution of work throughout the year has followed. The supposed need of dangerously long and irregular hours in the season trades are shown to be unnecessary. In place of alternating periods of intense overwork with periods of idleness, employers have found it possible to avoid such irregularities by foresight and management.

Report of Conference of Members of Women's Trade Unions on the Factory and Workshops Act, 1875. Vol. XXIX.

The permission granted to season trades for the extension of the hours to fourteen per day, during certain periods of the year, should be withdrawn, with the view of equalizing the work through-out the year. . . .

Bookbinders complained that the trade was most unnecessarily considered by the law a season trade. . . . The existence of the modification made employers careless of due economy in time. (Page 193.)

Report of the British Chief Inspector of Factories and Workshops, 1892.

I am convinced that there is no necessity for this overtime; the season-trade work or the press orders would be executed just the same if overtime were illegal, as it is in the textile and many of the non-textile trades; the work would only be spread over a longer period or mean the employment of more hands. Much of the good done by the Factory Act is undone by allowing delicate women and girls to work from 8 A. M. to 10 P. M. for two months of the year. (Page 89.)

Report of the British Chief Inspector of Factories and Workshops,
1892.

I believe that much of the apparent necessity for working overtime is simply the result of want of forethought and organization
on the part of employers and their managers. . . . How little
actual demand there is for overtime on the part of protected
hands, I think the return from this district will show. Out of
nearly nine thousand occupiers of factories and workshops, only
about two hundred apparently avail themselves of the permission
to work overtime; but then these two hundred have between them
made overtime on two thousand occasions during the year. (Page
88.)

Report of the British Chief Inspector of Factories and Workshops,
1900.

One of the most unsatisfactory results of the present system or
lack of system of working hours in laundries is the unfortunate
moral effect on the women and girls of this irregularity. The difficulty of securing steady regular work from employees and of en-
suring punctual attendance is complained of on all sides, and the
more intelligent employers are beginning to see that this is the
natural result of the irregularity in working hours. . . . Workers who on one or two days in the week are dismissed to idleness or
to other occupations, while on the remaining days they are expected to work for abnormally long hours, are not rendered methodical, industrious, or dependable workers by such an unsatisfactory training. The self-control and good habits engendered
by a regular and definite period of moderate daily employment,
which affords an excellent training for the young worker in all
organized industries, is sadly lacking, and, instead, one finds
periods of violent overwork alternating with hours of exhaustion.
The result is the establishment of a kind of " vicious circle "; bad
habits among workers make compliance by their employers with
any regulation as to hours very difficult. (Page 385.)

Report of the British Association for the Advancement of Science,
1902.

By forcing the employers to make their trade as regular as
possible, the overtime clauses have operated toward increased
efficiency. (Page 287.)

Report of the British Association for the Advancement of Science,
1903.

A very important, perhaps from the economic point of view the
most important, effect of legislation has been to spread the period
of work more uniformly through the week, month, and year than
had been the case before regulation. (Page 5.)

Restriction is met by adaptation of manufacture or rearrange-
ment of numbers employed and time at which work is done, women
being still employed at the work.

. . . Thus, it will be seen that the loss of overtime is not
necessarily a loss of work, but a redistribution (and an economical
one, too) of the times at which work is done, and does not therefore mean a loss in income, but a steadying and regulation of
income. (Page 13.)

C. *Adaptation of Customers to Shorter Hours*

Experience shows how the demands of customers yield
to the requirements of a fixed working day. When customers are obliged to place orders sufficiently in advance
to enable them to be filled without necessitating overtime work, compliance with this habit becomes automatic.

Factory and Workshops Acts Commission, 1875. *British Sessional Papers,* 1876. Vol. XXIX.

A very large number of the orders of customers (to printers,
milliners, dressmakers, etc.), which it has been usual to keep back
to the last minute and then throw upon the already fully-burdened
workers, not merely can be quite as easily given so as to have
plenty of time for their completion, but also will be so given, and
are in fact so given, when and so often as the customer is made
to recognize that he otherwise runs the risk of not having his
orders completed in time to suit his own convenience. . . .

We trust in time that the use of overtime in trades of this class
may be restricted down to the vanishing point. (Page 41.)

Report of the British Association for the Advancement of Science,
1903.

The tendency to put off giving orders to the last moment is
easily checked when the customer can be met with a universal legal
prohibition. (Page 7.)

History of Factory Legislation. HUTCHINS *and* HARRISON. 1903.

Tremenheere then took the opinion of certain of the merchants on this point, and found them much more favorable to the extension of the Factory Act. . . . A limitation of hours might, it was admitted, occasionally produce inconvenience, but this would by degrees adjust itself. Merchants would have to think of their orders a little beforehand. . . . One bleacher very candidly admitted that knowing the bleacher would undertake to bleach and finish one thousand pieces of cloth in five days he often, in cases of sudden orders, gave him only five days to do it in; but that, if the hours of the boys and women working were restricted so he would know the work could not be accomplished in that time, he should have to make his arrangements beforehand to give seven or .ten days, or to send part of the order to another bleacher. It was pointed out that if a bleacher lost part of an order on one occasion it would be made up to him on another, and that very possibly the bleachers would enlarge their works and keep more hands ready. If legislation were alike for all, the outlay would do the trade no harm. Tremenheere arrived at the conclusion that a limitation of women's and boys' hours would cause the masters to enlarge their works and improve their machinery rather than chance losing an order. . . . In 1857 . . . the mere anticipation of some such measure had caused additions to be made both to buildings and machinery which would considerably augment the firms' power of getting speedily through an increased quantity. (Page 134.)

D. *Incentive to Improvements in Manufacture*

The regulation of the working day has acted as a stimulus to improvement in processes of manufacture. Invention of new machinery and perfection of old methods have followed the introduction of shorter hours.

Report of the Wisconsin Bureau of Labor Statistics, 1903–1904.

Wherever a uniform standard of wages, hours of labor, and wholesome sanitary conditions have been uniformly enforced, the result has been that laborers have been stimulated to render greater services to their employers, and, in turn, employers strive to excel in improved machinery and devices for the protection of employees, sanitation, and methods of production in general. (Page 138.)

That the enforcing of a certain standard in regard to hours of labor, wages, and sanitary conditions compels employers to continually seek more improved machinery and methods of production is as true in practice as in theory. (Page 140.)

The Case for the Factory Acts. Edited by Mrs. SIDNEY WEBB. *London*, 1901.

But the exemption from regulation is also responsible for corresponding deficiencies in the technical administration of the industry. The very fact that the employers are legally free to make their operatives work without limit, and to crowd any number of them into one room, makes them disinclined to put thought and capital into improving the arrangements.

. . . We might indefinitely prolong the list of examples of the effect of the Factory Acts in improving the processes of manufacture. (Page 53.)

Woman in Industry. R. GONNARD. *Paris*, 1905.

The inspector of labor of Lyons says:

" It has come about that this decrease of the legal maximum limit of hours of labor (ten hours a day), which went into effect the 28th of March, 1902, obliging the employer to pay a higher wage for overtime hours, has urged the manufacturers to replace their former equipment by machines of great producing power. In short, for the manufacturers in question, the regulation has become a powerful stimulus, which has driven them to do away with methods of manufacture already somewhat superannuated." (Page 78.)

History of Factory Legislation. HUTCHINS *and* HARRISON. 1903.

If it could be shown that this regulated industry, far from suffering in competition with others, went ahead, improved its machinery, and developed a higher standard of comfort than its rivals, then, although the improvement might not be due to the legislation, there would be, at all events, a strong presumption that good and not harm had been done. And this is what has taken place. . . . The improvement in the regulated industry was clear and conspicuous. (Page 121.)

E. *Effect on Scope of Women's Employment*

The establishment of a legal limit to the hours of woman's labor does not result in contracting the sphere of her work.

Foreign Work and English Wages. By THOMAS BRASSEY, 1st *Baron Brassey. London,* 1879.

The argument that the tendency of the Factory Acts is to place an artificial restriction on the employment of women, and thus to depreciate the market value of this labor, is refuted on every hand by practical experience in the textile manufactories. Here the restrictions upon women's work are the most stringent, and yet the tendency for a long series of years has been the opposite — the proportion of women employed has steadily increased. The same observation applies to many of the trades and occupations carried on in London. As for the rate of wages paid, there is not an employer in the metropolis who will hesitate to acknowledge that there has been during the last ten or fifteen years a very substantial and important advance in the remuneration given to women for their work. (Pages 338, 339.)

The Case for the Factory Acts. Edited by MRS. SIDNEY WEBB. *London,* 1901.

But, it may be objected, that although Factory Legislation would improve the women, it annoys the employer, and makes him inclined to get rid of women altogether and employ men. As a matter of fact, this course, though often threatened beforehand, is not in practice followed. Where women can be employed, their labor is so much cheaper than that of men that there is no chance of their being displaced. The work of men and women tending automatically to differentiate itself into separate branches, it follows that there is very little direct competition between individual men and women. (Page 209.)

The Night-work of Women in Industry. PROF. E. BAUER. *Jena,*
1903.

All the official Swiss figures indicate that the establishment of
the normal, legal working day has never, or rarely, narrowed the
field of women's industrial activity. The restriction has exercised
upon the distribution of the classes of people who compose the
working world no notable influence.

The results show how unfounded were the fears cherished both
as to the loss for the working women of a part of their wage, and
the advantages which arise from the regulation of the working
day are, on the other hand, considerable for the whole body of the
workers. (Page 38.)

History of Factory Legislation. HUTCHINS *and* HARRISON. 1903.

It is surely extremely significant that whilst the attack on the
regulation of women's labor has been fruitless in better organized
industries — that is, in those which can make their wishes felt —
it has taken effect precisely in those industries which are unorganized and collectively inarticulate. By the admission of the opposition itself, the women whose trades have been under State control
for thirty, forty, or fifty years are now so strong, so efficient, so
well organized that even those who most strongly disapprove of
State control do not wish to withdraw it from them. Yet we are
to believe that to those who are still working long hours, in un-
sanitary conditions, State control would mean lowered wages, perhaps ruin! (Page 193.)

Women's Work and Wages. By EDWARD CADBURY. *London,* 1906.

This witness (Mr. Johnson, Sub-inspector of Factories) did not
think that the limitation of hours of women would lead to the
substitution of men for women, nor to any reduction of women's
wages. He did not consider that there were many trades where
men could be substituted for women, because of the nature of the
work. This was an intelligent and true forecast of what has
actually happened. (Page 36.)

It is often stated by those who oppose regulation of women's
work by legislation that the effect of such legislation is to displace
women in favor of men. Our inquiry seems to prove, however, that
this idea is erroneous, and that in the large majority of cases . . .

it is other questions altogether that determine the division of labor between men and women. A great deal of light has been thrown on the question of women's work and wages generally by the elucidation of the fact that as a rule men and women do different work, and the relation between men and women workers is, on the whole, that of two non-competing groups. It is quite true that that marginal division between the two groups is constantly shifting, but in the particular trades where this is the case the questions considered are the difference in wages between the two groups, their aptitude and physical fitness for certain work, and the fact that women expect to leave work when married. (Page 39.)

V. UNIFORMITY OF RESTRICTION

The arguments in favor of allowing overtime in seasonal trade or in cases of supposed emergency have gradually yielded to the dictates of experience which show that uniformity of restriction is essential to carrying out the purposes of the act.

A. *Allowance of Overtime Dangerous to Health*

Report of the British Chief Inspector of Factories and Workshops,
    1873.

To my mind it seems very fallacious reasoning to attempt to justify overtime amongst females . . . on the ground that, taking the year through, the hours of work average less than sixty weekly. A girl is not a whit less likely to be injured physically and morally by working fourteen hours a day in May and June because she has not to work more than seven hours in September and October. (Page 43.)

In regard to milliners and dressmakers, I strongly deprecate the granting of " fourteen-hour permissions," which only unsettle the trade, and are quite unnecessary. Such hours are very injurious to the girls employed. (Page 134.)

Report of the British Chief Inspector of Factories and Workshops,
    1898.

Sixty hours' actual work in a normal week may be considered as a reasonable amount by the average laundry girl, but when one day in the week is a whole holiday, prescribed by the Factory Act, and she is still required to work sixty hours in the remaining five days, she apparently seems to feel that she is not being fairly dealt by, and that the law is taking away with one hand what it gave with the other. Several complaints have been received of sixty hours' employment in a laundry on the five consecutive days following a statutory holiday, as of something illegal, and a visit paid in response to one of these on a Saturday following a Monday Bank (holiday) found manageress, women, and girls tired out and murmuring that a holiday which had to be made up for as they had made it up was no holiday. (Page 107.)

Report of the British Chief Inspector of Factories and Workshops, 1901.

It is often said that the rigidly fixed hours for work and meals in factories tend to make of the worker a machine, taking no actual personal interest in her work, while actually the effect is to help her, if the work does not occupy too great a part of the day, to be a person of some vigor interested in the work, but not entirely to the exclusion of other things, for which she can count on regular periods of leisure. (Page 178.)

B. *Uniformity Essential for Purposes of Enforcement*

In order to establish enforceable restrictions upon working hours of women, the law must fix a maximum working day. Without a fixed limit of hours, beyond which employment is prohibited, regulation is practically nullified. Exemptions of special trades from the restriction of hours not only subject the workers in such industries to injurious overwork, but go far to destroy the whole intent of the law.

The difficulties of inspection become insuperable.

The Case for the Factory Acts. Edited by Mrs. Sidney Webb. *London,* 1901.

To accede to the demand for greater elasticity is to suppose a higher code of morals on the part both of employers and of employed than experience justifies, and it would also render necessary a far more elaborate and irritating system of inspection than at present exists. The efficiency of modern factory industry depends very greatly upon automatic working — upon its standardization of conditions; and the existing factory law with its inelastic provisions is, in reality, a great aid in maintaining those conditions of efficiency. (Page 93.)

Report of the British Chief Inspector of Factories and Workshops,
1873.

From the point of view of one empowered to carry out the law,
I consider these modifications in favor of " season trades " as most
unfortunate. They immensely increase the difficulties of inspection, and it introduces an element of uncertainty and dissatisfaction into the relations between inspector and inspected, which cannot but be productive of ill results. For a law to be thoroughly
respected and obeyed, there should be no apparent partiality or
contradiction in its provisions, and if it is to work with ease and
efficiency these cannot be too completely simplified. (Page 134.)

Report of the British Chief Inspector of Factories and Workshops,
1873.

The difficulty of acquiring evidence, too, of this overwork is very
great, for the danger of loss of employment on the disclosure of
facts is so deterrent of exact information by the oppressed workers
that they will not appear before the magistrates to support the
Sub-Inspector in his attempt to protect them, however urgently or
indignantly that protection has been claimed. (Page 44.)

Report of the British Chief Inspector of Factories and Workshops,
1898.

Nothing has been more striking than the difficulties surround-
ing the law affecting laundries. The immensely long hours, the
absence of any conditions as to mealtimes other than that there
shall be at least half an hour in every five hours' spell, and the
extraordinary manner in which overtime is at present worked, com-
bine to make the inspection of laundries more difficult and more
ineffectual than in any trade I have had under my notice. (Page
107.)

Report of the British Chief Inspector of Factories and Workshops,
1900.

The existence of an exemption in the fish-curing trade has rendered the administration difficult and uncertain in result. It is
noteworthy that in this trade, in which overtime is permissible to
women on sixty occasions in the year, I have never found overtime
notices in use in any workshop. The occupiers do not find them

necessary. Starting with an exemption for one process, that of " gutting, salting, and packing," the industry would seem to have shaken itself gradually free from control, until now we find fish that have been in salt for several weeks dealt with as perishable articles. Given plenty of time and unsuitable surroundings, every article of food is to some extent perishable, and when a herring has been kept in salt for some weeks there is no reason for working on it at night except the reason that the day will bring other work, and in this seems to lie the cause of much of the late and irregular hours of the fish-curing trade. . . .

One of the evils to which this want of regulation leads is the practice of employing the same person in the same day in processes controlled by the Acts, and in those outside their control.

. . . In another case in which a curer had a factory and also a kippering shop in the same town, the workers went from one to the other, always sure of their full day's work in the factory, followed very often by five or six hours' work in the other shop. (Page 383.)

The Case for the Factory Acts. Edited by Mrs. Sidney Webb.
London, 1901.

The fact that exceptions lead always to illegalities — that a permission to work till ten at night leads constantly to work till one or two in the morning — appears frequently. (Page 153.)

Report of the British Chief Inspector of Factories and Work-shops, 1902.

After six years' experience of the effect of the present regulations, it is impossible not to feel greatly depressed by the result; the elasticity of the law has tended to encourage rather than check these unsettled hours. (Page 174.)

Labor Laws for Women in Germany. Dr. Alice Salomon. *Published by the Women's Industrial Council. London, 1907.*

Unfortunately, however, the law provides for a number of exceptions to the above rules respecting the hours of labor, exceptions which render adequate control difficult and greatly weaken the effect of the law. (Page 5.)

C. *Uniformity Essential to Justice to Employers*

To grant exceptions from the restriction of hours to certain industries places a premium upon irregularity and the evasion of law. When restrictions are uniform, the law operates without favor and without injury to individuals. Few employers are able to grant their employees reductions of hours, even if they are convinced of its advantages, when their competitors are under no such obligation. Justice to the employer as well as to the employee therefore requires that the law set a fixed limit of hours for working women and a limit fixed for all alike.

Report of the British Chief Inspector of Factories and Workshops, 1873.

In regard to " season trades " modification, the employers in favor of the modifications, argue, that it would be, firstly, a hardship upon them should they be unable to fulfil a large order unexpectedly coming in; that it would be calculated to drive their trade from them to others, either employing more workers or not at that time so busy.

To this I answer . . . that the hardship to themselves that the employers here complain of is only one which they would share in common with every other trader and manufacturer in the country, which are happily prevented by legislative enactment from gratifying their cupidity or caprice at the expense of others; and that the establishment of a uniform system of hours of labor would place all upon a more equal footing in the very matter complained of than in point of fact they are on now.

There can be no doubt that much uncertainty and dissatisfaction exists amongst trades generally at the granting unusual privileges to certain selected ones, and that this is a serious obstruction to the performance of the duties of inspection. (Page 134.)

Report of the Massachusetts Bureau of Labor Statistics, 1881.

As a further result, we have found that a large majority of the manufacturers would prefer ten hours to any greater number, " if only all would agree to it." Repeatedly has it occurred, when our agents have made known their errand, that almost the first words of the manufacturer would be, " It (ten hours) would be better for manufacturer and operative, if it could only be made universal "; and these words, always spoken so spontaneously as to show that they were the expression of a settled conviction, may be fairly taken to express the united wisdom of the manufacturers of textile fabrics in New York and New England. (Page 458.)

As one reason for this it was constantly said, that, if all worked but ten hours, then it would be the same for all, and so everybody would have just as fair a chance for success under ten as now under more hours. (Page 459.)

Report of the British Chief Inspector of Factories and Work-shops, 1900.

A lack of loyal adherence to reasonable hours of employment by many laundry occupiers increases the difficulty for those who make the attempt in real earnestness. Many employers gladly welcome further regulation as a means of organizing and controlling their workers. " What is the use of my making the effort to so organize my work that the laundry shall close at 8 P. M. like other reasonable work-places do," said a disheartened employer; " all the neighboring laundries are open until nine, ten, or even eleven o'clock, and my women find it suits their irregular habits to go and work in these places after they leave my premises; they are then too tired out to arrive at my laundry till 9.30 or 10 next morning. If we all had to keep the same rules and close at the same time, the law would work fairly; as it is I must just scramble on with the others in the stupid expensive old way." (Page 385.)

The Case for the Factory Acts. Edited by Mrs. Sidney Webb. London, 1901.

Now and again an employer complains of some hard experience, and forgets that a departure from rigid rule would destroy the certainty which he feels that the law is treating him exactly as it is his competitors. Such a feeling of security is essential to business enterprise. (Page 93.)

*Report of the British Chief Inspector of Factories and Work-
shops, 1902.*

I have discussed this matter with numbers of all classes concerned, even to those who are at present availing themselves to
the full of the concessions under the law, and with hardly any exceptions they have agreed that if we, as factory inspectors, could
insure that nowhere should the unprincipled be able to steal a
march on those who observed the law, and all overtime abolished,
they would be more than satisfied. They freely admit the evils
resulting from overtime, and these can be spoken to by all my col-
leagues, and I think in all large towns by the police. (Page 88.)

The innumerable loopholes and subterfuges which it affords to
a sharp and unscrupulous employer places his more stupid or more
scrupulous competitor at an unfair disadvantage, which is prevent-
able, and therefore should be prevented. The broad, clear limitations, easily understood and capable of being exactly and thoroughly enforced, which apply to other industries under the Act,
impose the same obligations and provide the same protection for
all alike. This is impossible where regulations cannot be properly
enforced and can be continually evaded with success. (Page 174.)

VI. THE REASONABLENESS OF THE TEN–HOUR DAY

Factory inspectors, physicians, and working women are unanimous in advocating the ten-hour day, wherever it has not yet been established. Some indeed consider ten hours too long a period of labor; but as opposed to the unregulated or longer day, there is agreement that ten hours is the maximum number of working hours compatible with health and efficiency.

A. *Opinions of Physicians and Officials*

British Sessional Papers. DR. LOUDON. 1833. Vol. XXI.

From fourteen (years of age) upwards, I would recommend that no individual should, under any circumstances, work more than twelve hours a day; although if practicable, as a physician, I would prefer the limitation of ten hours for all persons who earn their bread by industry. Ten working hours a day are in fact thirteen hours, allowing an hour for dinner, half an hour for breakfast, half an hour for tea-time, half an hour for going, and the same for returning from work. (Page 24.)

Report of Special Committee to inquire as to the Propriety of reducing the Hours of Labor. Massachusetts Legislative Document. House, 1865.

This (system of ten hours) is now very generally in use, — the exceptions being in manufacturing towns and corporations, — where they now require . . . women and children to work eleven hours daily — one hour more than in England — a disgrace in our opinion to Massachusetts and an outrage on humanity. (Page 2.)

Report of the Special Commission on the Hours of Labor. Massachusetts Legislative Documents. House, 1866, No. 98.

Dr. Tewksbury has been a practising physician eighteen years in Lawrence, and a close observer of the health and morals of operatives. Thinks long confinement in mills and insufficient time for meals injurious, and that ten hours a day is better than eleven or twelve hours.

Dr. Sargent, many years practising physician in Lawrence: Ten hours a day enough for strong men; too long for delicate women. (Page 63.)

Massachusetts Legislative Documents. House, 1867, No. 44.

I recommend, as the result of my investigations, and in view of the expressed wish of the interest of labor in the factories, . . . the enactment of ten hours as a legal standard for a day's labor. (Page 141.)

Conclusions and Recommendations. Massachusetts Bureau of Statistics of Labor, 1872.

1. That the hours of labor are too long [for women], and that the preliminary step to remedy the evil is the enactment of a law restricting labor in all manufacturing and mechanical establishments in the State to *ten hours per day* or to *sixty hours per week*. (Page 96.)

Report to the Local Governing Board on Proposed Changes in Hours and Ages of Employment in Textile Factories. By J. H. Bridges, M.D., and T. Holmes. British Sessional Papers. Vol. LV. 1873.

7. Q. Do you think that the present day's work (ten and one-half hours) is too long for young persons under twenty or for the grown-up women?

A. Yes. Nine and one-half hours appears sufficiently long for young persons under twenty, but eight hours would, *cæteris paribus*, more greatly conduce to their health.

For women over twenty, nine and one-half hours is a reasonable time so long as they remain unmarried. (Page 40.)

Factory and Workshops Act Commission, 1875. British Sessional Papers, 1876. Vol. XXIX. Appendix D. 87 c.

One of the evils arising from female labor is the numbers of hours they are allowed to work, being so many hours in excess of a great deal of male labor. We would suggest that all females, married and single, commence work not earlier than 8 A. M. and not work later than 7 P. M.

(Signed) EDWARD BENNETT.
SAUL HINGLEY.

Pennsylvania. Annual Report of Secretary of Internal Affairs. Part III. Industrial Statistics, 1880–1881. Vol. IX.

The agitation of the ten-hour system among the working people of this State began as far back as 1834 and 1835, extending through many years. The custom of working twelve and thirteen hours per day became exceedingly obnoxious to the working classes, and great efforts were made to prevail upon proprietors to reduce the number of hours to ten per day. . . . Injury to health, no time for leisure, recreation, or study, a total deprivation of social and innocent pleasure, by an all-work and bed system, was the great plea of the laborer, while the stereotyped objection of the employer was, that a reduction of the hours would curtail production, and thus render them unable to compete with like establishments in other sections of the country. (Page 100.)

That ten hours per day is fully as much as should be exacted from the employees we think cannot be gainsaid, and such is the spirit of the law, as well as the sentiments of all who take an interest in promoting the welfare of mankind in general and of labor in particular. The justice of both law and sentiment becomes more apparent when we contemplate the class of labor employed in factories and their relation to future generations. To the strong and sturdy male adult the task of being compelled to labor more than ten hours per day might not seem arduous, more especially where the work assigned to him is not of such a character as to be a drain upon his physical constitution; but, while this exception may possibly be granted, its compulsory exaction from the large number of women, girls, and young children employed admits of no excuse. In the returns received by the Bureau, the number of women and girls over fifteen years of age employed are 23,076; boys under sixteen, 4,183, and 3,548 girls under fifteen. . . .

These figures, without special analysis, we presume are sufficient to convince the most sceptical of the wisdom of a systematic enforcement of the ten-hour law by proper legislation, to the end that youth be protected, the condition of life be ameliorated, and the future of our State be promoted. Nor should the law be confined to factories alone, but extended to all industries where women and children are in any manner apt to be employed to the detriment of life and health. (Page 104.)

Condition of Female Labor in Toronto. By Jean Thompson Scott. 1891.

The clause in the Act which allows a different apportionment of the hours per day in case of shorter hours on Saturday is an unfortunate one, because it would permit an average of eleven hours a day for five days in the week — far too long a period for women to work. (Page 29.)

Report of the Maine Bureau of Industrial and Labor Statistics, 1892.

In view of all the facts in the case, we were led to accept the ten-hour day, and it has proved a better day for all concerned than the twelve or fourteen hour day. In many industries the workers are employed at piece work, and do not average over eight hours a day, and in this they simply follow natural law and stop work when they feel that a good day's work has been accomplished and feel so tired as to need rest or change. (Page 11.)

Report of the German Imperial Factory Inspectors, 1895.

For adult working women, with very few exceptions, the eleven-hour working day is the rule. In Würzburg several establishments have ten hours. In the length of the working day there is no conspicuous difference between factories and workshops (Aschaffenburg).

As to the customary working hours in Hamburg the following summary is enlightening. The working day of women varies from eight to eleven hours.

8	hours and less in 10	places with	115	women.
8–8½	"	"	"	" 18	"	"	270	"
8½–9	"	"	"	" 44	"	"	984	"
9–9½	"	"	"	" 76	"	"	712	"
9½–10	"	"	"	" 77	"	"	1493	"
10½–11	"	"	"	" 54	"	"	802	"

Report of the New York Department of Factory Inspection, 1897.

Any woman employed at manual labor for ten consecutive hours per day, and constantly employed, is performing a task beyond her strength, whether she is just under or over twenty-one years of age. (Page 25.)

Report of the Commission Supérieure du Travail. Paris, 1897.

Twelve hours of steady work is an exertion which any young girls or women cannot often repeat except at the expense of health. The result of overtime work in the evening for a woman of any age is physical deterioration when it does not lead to moral deterioration as well. (Page 100.)

Report of the New York Bureau of Labor Statistics, 1900.

From that time (1881) to this, public opinion in Massachusetts has upheld the ten-hour law, and approved the extension of its principles. (Page 53.)

Industrial Conference National Civic Federation, 1902.

The most striking fact about this question of hours of labor seems to me its universality. In virtually every country dominated by Western civilization the daily work-time in mechanical industries is being cut down by successive movements that appear to be as inevitable as the tide, and that have the appearance of steps in the path of human progress. . . . (George Gunton, page 190.)

That the time is now ripe for another general reduction in the daily working time is indicated by the testimony of physicians and the mortality statistics of occupations. Medical research shows that a ten-hour day in modern industry calls for an expenditure of either muscular or nervous energy or both — depending upon the nature of the work — that inevitably shortens life. (A. F. Weber, Chief Statistician, New York Department of Labor, page 200.)

Report of the California Bureau of Labor Statistics, 1904.

A suggestion is made, which it is hoped will have the serious consideration of the people and of the legislators of the State; and it is, namely, that an amendment be made to the Constitution of California, providing, as is done by the Constitution of Massachusetts regarding that State, that our legislature shall, by appropriate legislation, provide for the health and welfare of women wage-earners in this State.   (Page 133.)

The Working Hours of Female Factory-hands. From the Reports of Factory Inspectors, collated in the Imperial Home Office. Published by VON DECKER. *Berlin,* 1905.

The inspector for Breslau says, " The reduction of the working day to ten hours is such a decided step in advance, and is of such marked and wholesome influence on the mental, physical, and moral status of the entire working population, that its introduction should be emphatically urged."

The inspector for Cologne says, " The reduction of the working day for all women over sixteen years must be regarded as a necessity for both moral and hygienic reasons."

The inspector for Hanover says, " The reasons for the reduction of the working day to ten hours —

(*a*) The physical organization of woman,
(*b*) Her maternal functions,
(*c*) The rearing and education of the children,
(*d*) The maintenance of the home —

are all so important and so far reaching that the need for such education need hardly be discussed."

Another inspector says, " Considering the detrimental physical defect of factory work, its nerve-exhausting character, its ruinous influence on family life, and the care of children, and, indeed, under all the aspects of the physical, moral, and mental development of the working class, the reduction of the legal working day for women must be regarded as an emphatic demand and a moral obligation, whose introduction must be urged after a careful and conscientious weighing of all the reasons for and against it."   (Page 106.)

Report of the Washington Bureau of Labor Statistics, 1905–1906.

The present law prohibits the employment of any female worker for a longer period than ten hours in any one calendar day.   Splendid results have been obtained through the operation of this law, for much as one may dislike to credit it, there are employers who would insist upon working their female help from twelve to sixteen hours per day did the law not stand in their way.

There is peculiar necessity for protecting through legislative means those classes of female workers who are employed in laundries, factories, and other similar industries. Eight hours of continuous work of that character is as much as should be exacted from any woman, and there is general agreement among those who have investigated the subject that the well-being of the community would be consulted through the adoption of an eight-hour day for all women employed in such occupations. (Page 18.)

The Case of the Factory Acts. Edited by Mrs. Sidney Webb. *London*, 1901.

No one who studies the actual working of the Factory Code can doubt that it will be perfected just in the measure in which all these differences are abolished and an equal adequacy of protection extended to all the places and all the persons who work. The ideal is that the regulations of all places in which manufacturing work for gain is carried on should approximate as closely as possible to those which obtain in the most completely guarded places, namely, the textile factories . . . the textile factory is cursed by no such overtime exception as elsewhere undermines the value of the hours' limitation.

The overtime exception is doomed. Unless some unforeseen change in our industrial conditions revolutionizes the present order of things, the total abolition of overtime for women must follow on that for young persons, which was virtually accomplished by Mr. Asquith in 1895. . . . The case for abolition was as clearly proved as the complete consensus of opinion on the subject of those who work under the exception and those who have to enforce it could prove anything. The opinions of H. M. Inspectors of Factories and the opinions of the organized women workers were all but unanimous against allowing any overtime. These opinions, the expression of which dates back to the Royal Commission of 1875, are based on arguments which carry with them conviction on many grounds. Over and over again the view is stated that with better organization of the business the need for overtime disappears. Cases are quoted to prove that many large dressmaking and millinery firms never avail themselves of this exception, and the great object lesson of the textile trade is given. In all textile factories, and in a great many non-textile factories, to which no exception has been granted, organization and management quite easily cope with the recurring season pressure, and the trade automatically adapts itself to the law's requirements. In other non-textile factories and workshops, to which the overtime exception has been extended, demands no more urgent are met by the deliberate overtaxing of the workers' health and strength. (Page 153.)

In 1878, when this industry (fruit-preserving (jam-making) factories) was first brought under inspection, the employers protested against any regulation of the hours of labor, or even of sanitation, during the jam-making season, on the plea that the fruit had to be dealt with as it was delivered. The House of Commons, instead of insisting that the employers should exert their brains so as to cope with difficulties inherent in their particular trade, weakly accepted their plea, and exempted them from the Common Rules enforced on other industries. What has been the result? The majority of British jam factories at the beginning of the twentieth century present, during the summer months, scenes of overwork, overcrowding, dirt and disorder, hardly to be equalled by the cotton mills at the beginning of the nineteenth century. Women and young girls are kept continuously at work week-days and Sundays alike; often as much as a hundred hours in the seven days; and sometimes for twenty or even thirty hours at a stretch.

. . . As if on purpose to complete the proof that these shortcomings are not inevitable in the business, and are merely the result of a disastrous exemption from regulation, we have the fact that, here and there, in different parts of the kingdom, a few firms stand out as preferring the " upward way "; scientifically organizing their supplies, providing cold storage, working their operatives only normal hours, and seeing to it that the work-places are clean and healthy. If the " downward way " were barred by law, as it is in cotton-spinning, all jam-making firms would long ago have been forced into the same course. (Page 50.)

B. *Opinions of Employees*

History of Factory Legislation. HUTCHINS *and* HARRISON.

In June, 1847, after the Bill became a law the rejoicings throughout the manufacturing districts were such as had never been known before. (Page 96.)

In order to test the general feeling, 10,270 adult male laborers in ten factories were examined as to their views on the question, and of these seventy per cent declared for a ten-hours day (for women and young persons) even though it might involve a reduction in wages. (Page 99.)

Report of the Massachusetts Bureau of Labor Statistics, 1871.

I have worked what is called ten hours a day, and the ten-hour system always has a good influence on the work-people. We don't lose one-eleventh of the pay, everybody knows that. I did n't lose a single cent, because I did n't get so much exhausted. . . . (Page 498.)

To prove the soundness of the ten-hour claim, the operatives instance the reduction in the past, from sixteen to fourteen, to thirteen and to twelve, and from twelve to eleven hours. They also point to the twenty-one years' experience in Great Britain, where the reduction was made in 1850 from twelve to ten, a reduction of one-sixth of the working day. (Pages 557–558.)

Report of the British Chief Inspector of Factories and Workshops, 1877.

" Since the meeting of the Trades Union Congress at Leicester, however, I have made it my business to ascertain, so far as I could, the opinion of women employed in different occupations in London as to the influence of the Factory Acts, and I can say confidently that without a single exception I have found the limitations imposed upon their hours of work most cordially approved of, and the greatest anxiety and positive alarm entertained at the prospect of any relaxation which would expose them to the irregular and uncertain hours of work which prevailed prior to the passing of the Factory Act of 1867. Among what class of working-women of London it can be pretended that the regulations and restrictions imposed by the Factory Acts are unpopular, I confess I am altogether at a loss to understand. All I can say is that notwithstanding most diligent inquiry I have entirely failed to meet with them. . . ."

A—— F—— states: " . . . I decidedly prefer to work the hours fixed by the Factory Acts. After working as a book-folder for about five years I left, as I found the long and irregular hours made me ill. I have never had any illness since the Factory Act came into operation. The general opinion among the women in the shop is that they prefer working under the Factory Act, and they grumble much when they are kept later than eight o'clock."

E—— B——, a book sewer, says: " I have been six years employed in the sewing department. I am very well satisfied with the Factory Acts as they are, and I think all the sewers are of opinion that it is a good law, as it prevents excessive overwork. I had no experience of the trade before the passing of the Factory Act, but from what I have been told, the state of things must have been dreadful. I have never heard any of the women complain of the Factory Act in any way, nor of its preventing them from getting employment; and as far as I can judge, the number of women employed in the book-binding trade is increasing." (Pages 12, 13.)

Report of the Massachusetts Bureau of Labor Statistics, 1881.

What is the greatest desire of the factory operatives? We reply, Beyond all question, one of the greatest desires of the factory operatives of America, relative to employment, is for ten hours. . . . We have examined hundreds, a large part of them overseers, and altogether the greater part of them are in favor of ten hours anyway, let the pay come as it will. (Page 464.)

Report of Connecticut Bureau of Labor Statistics, 1888.

The law forbidding the employment of women and children for more than ten hours per day, or sixty hours per week, has met with general public favor. In a majority of cases the law is conscientiously obeyed. (Page 25.)

Report of the Connecticut Bureau of Labor Statistics, 1890.

. . . The violation of this law is objected to by the most of the working people, on the ground that ten hours out of twenty-four make as long a day as women and children should ever be required to work. (Page 29.)

Report of the German Imperial Factory Inspectors, 1895.

In regard to efforts made to abolish female labor in factories, the inspector for the Dresden district remarks: " Among the workers themselves, even married women, there is no emphatic desire to prohibit industrial work for women, *provided that* this labor was subject to certain limitations, — did not occur at night or on Sundays, and did not last more than ten hours by day." (Page 93.)

Report of the German Imperial Factory Inspectors, 1895.

" For the working-women, even for those who suffer loss of wages, the ten-hours day on Saturday, closing at 5.30 is very welcome, as they have stated in numerous cases, and there is no doubt that the law meets the wishes of the workers." (Page 150.)

Report of the New York Bureau of Labor Statistics, 1900.

We have thus seen how industrial efficiency has been improved to such an extent by legislative restrictions upon the hours of labor that the maximum length of the working day for women and minors has been successively reduced until it is nine and one-half in England and virtually the same in Massachusetts (fifty-eight hours a week), and that the extension of such legislation has been, and still is, desired by the operatives themselves, who would naturally be the principal sufferers if such a policy really meant diminished production. (Page 58.)

Labor Laws for Women in Germany. Dr. Alice Salomon. Published by Women's Industrial Council. London, 1907.

A chief means to this end, desired not merely by the women of Germany, but by most of her great political parties, is the reduction of the maximum working day to ten hours (to start with), a demand long since ripe for settlement, which has been proved practicable by enquiries of a Government Commission. For this concession working-women have already fought many a hard battle, and it ought no longer to be withheld from them, especially in view of the fact that most firms employing women have already adopted the ten-hours day, so that the legal enforcement of this measure would merely compel backward employers to bring their establishments up to date. (Page 9.)

C. *Opinions of Employers*

Report of the German Imperial Factory Inspectors, 1884.

Report for the Rhine Province, District of Dusseldorf — Dr. Wolf:

The question as to the length of the working day and as to whether it should be regulated by the State has been much discussed.

At a meeting at Gladbach of Textile Manufacturers it was resolved
" that the length of the working day can be effectively regulated
only by the laws of the country, and that such regulation should
be urged." (Page 150.)

Report of the German Imperial Factory Inspectors, 1888.

The report for the district of Chemnitz says that the manufacturers of that district have repeatedly expressed a desire for the
introduction of the ten-hour day. (Page 114.)

United States Industrial Commission, 1900.

We may find that it is desirable in time to do by law what a few
persons are doing voluntarily. It is in that way that the original
ten-hour law was tried tentatively in England; a few manufacturers tested the matter in their own factories and found that their
people could do as much in ten hours as they theretofore had been
doing in twelve and thirteen; that made the law seem reasonable.
(Page 64.)

Women in the Printing Trade. Edited by J. R. MacDonald.
London, 1904.

Some employers, like Mr. Bell, admit candidly enough that legislation enables them to be more humane (and humanity in this respect pays) than they could otherwise afford to be. The Act is
" a great relief," such an employer has said. " Legislation is an
excellent thing; existing hours are quite long enough. If a person
has not done her work by the time they are up, she never will do it."
" The Factory Acts are a very good thing," another has said. . . .
" Legislation is a very good thing. I don't believe in long hours.
Employers are often shortsighted and think that workers are like
machines — the longer you work them the more they do; but this
is not really the case; if they work from nine to seven they have
done as much as they are good for." " The good done by the Factory Acts has quite outweighed any evils or hardships." (Page
82.)

VII. LAUNDRIES

The specific prohibition in the Oregon Act of more than ten hours' work in laundries is not an arbitrary discrimination against that trade. Laundries would probably not be included under the general terms of " manufacturing " or " mechanical establishments "; and yet the special dangers of long hours in laundries, as the business is now conducted, present strong reasons for providing a legal limitation of the hours of work in that business.

A. *Present Character of the Business*

Massachusetts Bureau of Statistics of Labor. 1872.

Laundries: Much of this work is very fatiguing, and but few are able to endure the labor from month to month. (Page 96.)

Dangerous Trades. THOMAS OLIVER, *Medical Expert on Dangerous Trades Committees of the Home Office.* 1902. *Chapter XLVII. Laundry Workers.*

It is perhaps difficult to realize that the radical change which has everywhere transformed industrial conditions has already affected this occupation (laundry work) also, and that for good or for evil the washerwoman is passing under the influences which have so profoundly modified the circumstances of her sister of the spinning-wheel and the sewing needle. When the first washing machine and ironing roller were applied to this occupation, alteration in the conditions became as much a foregone conclusion as it did in the case of the textile or the clothing manufactures, when the spinning frame, the power loom, or the sewing machine appeared.

Meanwhile, few industries afford at the present time a more interesting study. From a simple home occupation it is steadily being transformed by the application of power-driven machinery and by the division of labor into a highly organized factory industry, in which complicated labor-saving contrivances of all kinds play a prominent part. The tremendous impetus in the adoption of machinery, and the consequent modification of the system of employment so striking in the large laundries, is not greater than the less obvious but even more important development in the same direction among small laundries. Indeed the difference is rapidly becoming one of degree only. In the large laundries may be found perhaps more machinery and a greater number of the newest devices, but the fundamental change has affected all alike.

" With this advent of machinery and subdivision of labour, the whole character of the industry has changed. It is becoming more and more evident that, from the smallest to the largest laundry, the industry is passing — has indeed in some respects already passed — out of the peculiar position which it has hitherto occupied, and is taking its place alongside ordinary trades." [1]

The manufacture of laundry machinery, to which much energy and capital is devoted, is every year increasing. New and ingenious inventions and improvements constantly appear, many of which come from America, whence a considerable amount of this machinery is imported.

The " calender machine " has been adapted to laundry work, and is now commonly found in quite small laundries; it consists of huge steam or gas heated cylinders, varying from four to eight or nine feet long, either revolving singly in a metal bed, as in the case of the " decoudun," or on each other, as in the case of the multiple-roller calenders. The linen is generally drawn in under the hot, revolving rollers, which thus " iron " it smooth and glossy, a cloud of steam arising as each damp article passes under the roller. Constant care is required to so put the work under the machine that the hands are not also drawn under; want of attention may be followed by an accident, and even where care is exercised the fingers may be entangled in a string or hole in the material and the hand thus drawn in. The heat given off by these machines is sometimes very great; a temperature of over 90° F. may be registered even in winter on the feeding-step in front of this machine. . . . at which little girls stand all day long. (Pages 663–666.)

This work is not the light and often pleasant occupation of sewing or folding. It is not done sitting down. From morning to night these young girls are constantly standing; they are generally tending machines, the majority of which are specially heated, and they work in an atmosphere in which steam, which

[1] Annual Report of the Chief Inspector of Factories for 1900.

is nearly always present, makes the high temperature far more oppressive than would be the case if the air were not thus artificially saturated to an excessive degree with moisture. Steam rises from the calenders and various machines. It is given off also by the damp clothes, which in many laundries, even large ones, hang drying or airing overhead or on " horses " in the room. The conditions in this respect are often at least as trying as in any spinning-mill, and the hours during which the girls are exposed to them very much longer. (Page 670.)

Colorado. Third Biennial Report of the Bureau of Labor Statistics, 1891–1892. Part II. Female Wage Earners.

In some laundries the hours of employment during the rush frequently extend to eleven and twelve hours per day, although no extra compensation is paid to female employees, with but few exceptions. . . . While machinery to a large extent relieves her (the female laundry worker) of much work, the full strength of her physical endurance is taxed by a tedious attention to the duties assigned her. (Page 28.)

B. *Bad Effect upon Health*

Report of British Chief Inspector of Factories and Workshops, 1900.

The whole work of a laundry is done standing, and the practice of so apportioning the legal " sixty hours a week " that on three or four days in the week the women have to work from 8 A. M. to 10 or 11 at night — a practice which could be, and where there is proper organization often is, rendered needless — has its natural result in the form of disease to which laundry workers are extremely liable. It is well known that they suffer much from varicose veins, and terrible ulcers on the legs ; but the extraordinary extent to which they are so afflicted is, I think, not generally known. In many other trades standing is a necessary condition, and it is difficult to account for the far greater prevalence of this disease among laundry workers than among others of the same class engaged in ordinary factory occupations, except on the ground of the long and irregular hours. (Page 383.)

With a view to arriving, if possible, at some definite knowledge of the position of laundry workers as compared with other women of their class and situation, in regard to the question of health, I have this year devoted some time to inquiring into the

subject in the districts under my charge and in neighboring
localities. . . . By the kindness of the superintendents of the two
first infirmaries (Islesworth, and Wandsworth and Clapham) I
have been able to examine the carefully kept records of the number,
ages, occupations, and diseases of the patients. The following
tables, compiled from these records, speak for themselves, and
afford some indication of the kinds of disease to which laundry
workers appear to be particularly liable. (Page 384.)

TABLE A. ISLESWORTH INFIRMARY

(Includes Acton, Chiswick, Brentford — a typical laundry district)

	No.	Suffering from ulcers on the legs.	Per cent.	Phthisis.	Proportion.
1898 Laundresses . . .	58	9	1 in 6	6	1 in 10
Women, other than laundresses . .	179	7	1 in 25	7	1 in 25
1899 Laundresses . . .	79	13	1 in 6	9	1 in 9
Women, other than laundresses . .	218	7	1 in.31	11	1 in 20

TABLE B. WANDSWORTH AND CLAPHAM INFIRMARY

(Includes Battersea — another laundry district)

	No.	Ulcers on the legs.	Proportion.	Rheumatism.	Proportion.	Bronchitis.	Proportion.	Phthisis.	Proportion.
1899 Laundresses	247	36	1 in 6	16	1 in 16	45	1 in 5	21	1 in 11
Women, other than laundresses	1171	50	1 in 23	49	1 in 22	129	1 in 9	63	1 in 19
1900 Laundresses	199	27	1 in 7	12	1 in 16	21	1 in 9	18	1 in 11
Women, other than laundresses	1127	41	1 in 27	69	1 in 16	133	1 in 9	59	1 in 19

108

At the Fulham and Hammersmith Infirmary about the same proportions exist, but it was not so easy to collect accurate statistics. . . . The figures supplied by the records of the cases attended by the Kensington District Nursing Association show a large proportion of ulcerated legs and of forms of internal disease aggravated by standing for long hours. I was struck by the absence of any particular liability to skin disease . . . noticed . . . some years ago, but . . . since almost disappeared. The immensely increased use of machinery in the process of washing . . . may account for this difference.

The constant exposure to steam, standing on wet floors, the great heat in which the work is carried on, and the long hours at exhausting work, amply explains the tendency to pulmonary disease. The badly arranged floors in large wash-houses are a constant source of discomfort and probably of ill-health to the workers. . . . It is not uncommon to find that the yellow and foul water from a row of tanks or washing machines at one side of a wash-house flows all across the floor and over the feet of the workers before eventually reaching the drain. . . . (Page 385.)

Dangerous Trades. THOMAS OLIVER, M.D., *Medical Expert of the Dangerous Trades Committee of the Home Office.* 1902.

It is impossible that the heat and steam, the exhausting manual labour (all of which is done standing), and above all the excessively long hours of work in this ill-regulated industry, can fail to have a marked effect on the health of the workers as a class. In 1893 and 1894, when inquiry as to these conditions preceded the passing of the Act of 1895, the periods of work of women and young girls were found to be excessively long — and they are still not only very long, but extraordinarily irregular. The most immediately obvious effect on health is to be found in the prevalence among these workers of ulcers on the legs and varicose veins. It would perhaps be hardly credited by any who are not intimately acquainted with them to what extent these poor women suffer in this respect. To stand at work all day is the lot of many industrial workers, but in no other woman's industry is this form of suffering so serious. In certain well-defined laundry districts in West London an inquiry at the Poor Law Infirmaries, to which, and not to the hospitals, the poor woman suffering from this troublesome and painful ailment most naturally resort, demonstrated the peculiar liability of laundry workers in this respect.

Ironers suffer from headaches and sore eyes, which result from constantly bending over the gas-heated irons in general use. The fumes from the tiny gas-jets — unless these and the air supply to each iron are very carefully regulated — are disagreeably noticeable on entering the room, and sometimes even the laundry, and are of course worst of all just above the iron so heated.

It would be interesting to test the accuracy of this general impression, which is shared by many medical and philanthropic persons who are interested in laundry workers, if figures were available on which to base a calculation of the " expectation of life " among these women. " Worn out while still young " is the expression constantly used by those whose professional work brings them into contact with these women when speaking of the effect of the occupation on health. (Pages 668–671.)

C. *Bad Effect on Safety*

Report of British Chief Inspector of Factories and Workshops,
   1903.

The comparative immunity from accidents in the laundries in the West Riding of Yorkshire may be possibly due in some measure to the moderate hours of employment.

The incidents of accidents according to time of day is somewhat surprising, the most dangerous hours apparently being 11 A. M. to 12 noon and 4 to 6 P. M. . . . Probably 11 A. M. to 12 noon is more generally than any other time the last tiring hour of a day five hours' spell; 4–6 P. M. covers the time when most generally the transition from daylight to artificial light. (Page 210.)

Reference was also made (in the Thirteenth International Congress of Hygiene), although figures were not adduced, to the alleged increase in the number of accidents which occur late in the working day when the effect of intellectual and physical fatigue have made themselves apparent. (Page 298.)

D. *Bad Effect upon Morals*

Report of British Chief Inspector of Factories and Workshops,
   1900.

One of the most unsatisfactory results of the present system or lack of system of working hours in laundries is the unfortunate moral effect on the women and girls of this irregularity. The difficulty of securing steady regular work from employees and of insuring punctual attendance is complained of on all sides, and the more intelligent employers are beginning to see that this is the natural result of the irregularity in working hours, which is still too readily fostered by many who do not realize its mischievous effect. Women who are employed at arduous work till far into the night are not likely to be early risers nor given to punctual attendance in the mornings, and workers who on one or two days in the week are dismissed to idleness or to other occupations, while on the remaining days they are expected to work for abnormally long hours, are not rendered methodical, industrious, or dependable workers by such an unsatisfactory training. The self-control and good habits engendered by a regular and definite period of moderate daily employment, which affords an excellent training for the young worker in all organized industries, is sadly lacking, and, instead, one finds periods of violent over-work alternating with hours of exhaustion. The result is the establishment of a kind of "vicious circle"; bad habits among workers make compliance by their employers with any regulation as to hours very difficult, while a lack of loyal adherence to reasonable hours of employment by many laundry occupiers increases the difficulty for those who make the attempt in real earnestness. (Page 386.)

Dangerous Trades. Thomas Oliver, M.D., *Medical Expert to Dangerous Trades Committee of the Home Office.* 1902.

The ten minutes or quarter-hour "lunch" of "beer" is common, and the "beer-man" who goes his rounds at 10 A. M. and 6 or 7 P. M. to all the laundries, delivering his cans of beer from the nearest public house, is an institution which is, I believe, unknown in any other trade. Imagine the amazement of the master of a mill or weaving factory if his employees were to stop in a body for a quarter of an hour twice a day between meals to drink beer! Yet in many laundries the beer is kept on the premises for the purpose, and it is certain that as long as time thus wasted (to put it on the lowest grounds) can be made up by each separate woman "working it out" at the end of the day, irregular dawdling and intemperate habits will be encouraged. On the other hand, a woman who is expected on Thursdays or Fridays to be in the laundry from 8 or 8.30 in the morning till 9 or 10 or 11 at night may claim with some show of reason that only by some kind of spur can she keep her over-tired body from flagging.

E. *Irregularity of Work*

Debate in the British House of Lords on Clause 30, *Factory and Workshops Bill. Hansards' Parliamentary Debates,* 1890–1891. Vol. CCCLV.

THE EARL OF DUNRAVEN. . . . But the hours that the women work (in laundries) are excessively long . . . I know it has been said, and it may be repeated in your Lordships' House, that this business is in the nature of a season trade; that there comes a sudden rush of work, and that it cannot be performed and the business carried on unless those employed in it work excessively long hours. Believe me, that is all nonsense. It may be the cause at the present time; but if the hours are limited, as they ought to be, the trade would very soon adapt itself to the new conditions. . . . Of course, my noble friend on the cross benches (Lord Wemyss) may be perfectly right in saying that it is a mistake altogether to interfere with the liberty of adult women; but if so, let us at least be consistent and do away with all our factory legislation affecting adult women. But if our factory legislation interfering with adult women is beneficial, as I believe it to be, then why . . . should it not be extended to these women who are engaged in this laborious work. (Page 1034.)

THE MARQUESS OF RIPON. . . . Then as to hours . . . surely in regard to work that is so hard and so laborious these poor women (laundresses) have just as good a claim to have their hours regulated as have the milliners and women employed in bootmakers' establishments, who are brought under the regulations of the Factories and Workshops Act. . . . Some of the noble Lords who have addressed the House have spoken as if our factory legislation was a thing to be deprecated and not extended. I believe it to be, as my noble friend behind me (Lord Sandhurst) said, one of the most successful portions of the legislation of this country. (Page 1038.)

Report of the British Chief Inspector of Factories and Work-shops, 1902.

The work of endeavoring to administer the regulation as to period of employment in (laundries) is extremely disheartening when work is carried on in spurts, the shamefully long hours, straining endurance to the utmost, alternating with days of idleness; the worker cannot be expected to develop any qualities but those of the casual laborer.   (Page 174.)

CONCLUSION

We submit that in view of the facts above set forth and of legislative action extending over a period of more than sixty years in the leading countries of Europe, and in twenty of our States, it cannot be said that the Legislature of Oregon had no reasonable ground for believing that the public health, safety, or welfare did not require a legal limitation on women's work in manufacturing and mechanical establishments and laundries to ten hours in one day.

See *Holden* v. *Hardy*, 169 U. S. 366, 395, 397.

LOUIS D. BRANDEIS,
Counsel for State of Oregon.

Boston, *January*, 1908.

Supreme Court of the United States

CURT MULLER,	IN ERROR TO
PLAINTIFF IN ERROR,	THE SUPREME COURT
v.	OF
THE STATE OF OREGON	THE STATE OF OREGON

FEBRUARY 24, 1908

MR. JUSTICE BREWER delivered the opinion of the Court.

On February 19, 1903, the legislature of the State of Oregon passed an act (Session Laws, 1903, p. 148) the first section of which is in these words:

" Sec. 1. That no female (shall) be employed in any mechanical establishment, or factory, or laundry in this State more than ten hours during any one day. The hours of work may be so arranged as to permit the employment of females at any time so that they shall not work more than ten hours during the twenty-four hours of any one day."

Section 3 made a violation of the provisions of the prior sections a misdemeanor, subject to a fine of not less than $10 nor more than $25. On September 18, 1905, an information was filed in the Circuit Court of the State for the county of Multnomah, charging that the defendant " on the 4th day of September, A. D. 1905, in the county of Multnomah and State of Oregon, then and there being the owner of a laundry, known as the Grand Laundry, in the city of Portland, and the employer of females therein, did

then and there unlawfully permit and suffer one Joe Haselbock, he, the said Joe Haselbock, then and there being an
overseer, superintendent and agent of said Curt Muller, in
the said Grand Laundry, to require a female, to wit, one
Mrs. E. Gotcher, to work more than ten hours in said
Laundry on said 4th day of September, A. D. 1905, contrary
to the statutes in such cases made and provided, and against
the peace and dignity of the State of Oregon."

A trial resulted in a verdict against the defendant, who
was sentenced to pay a fine of $10. The Supreme Court
of the State affirmed the conviction (48 Ore. 252), where-
upon the case was brought here on writ of error.

The single question is the constitutionality of the statute
under which the defendant was convicted so far as it affects
the work of a female in a laundry. That it does not conflict
with any provisions of the State constitution is settled by
the decision of the Supreme Court of the State. The con-
tentions of the defendant, now plaintiff in error, are thus
stated in his brief:

" (1) Because the statute attempts to prevent persons,
sui juris, from making their own contracts, and thus vio-
lates the provisions of the Fourteenth Amendment, as
follows:

" ' No State shall make or enforce any law which shall
abridge the privileges or immunities of citizens of the
United States; nor shall any State deprive any person of
life, liberty, or property, without due process of law; nor
deny to any person within its jurisdiction the equal protection of the laws.'

" (2) Because the statute does not apply equally to all
persons similarly situated, and is class legislation.

" (3) The statute is not a valid exercise of the police
power. The kinds of work prescribed are not unlawful,
nor are they declared to be immoral or dangerous to the
public health; nor can such a law be sustained on the
ground that it is designed to protect women on account of
their sex. There is no necessary or reasonable connection

between the limitation prescribed by the act and the public
health, safety, or welfare."

It is the law of Oregon that women, whether married or
single, have equal contractual and personal rights with
men. As said by Chief Justice Wolverton, in *First National Bank* v. *Leonard*, 36 Ore. 390, 396, after a review of
the various statutes of the State upon the subject:

" We may therefore say with perfect confidence that,
with these three sections upon the statute book, the wife can
deal, not only with her separate property, acquired from
whatever source, in the same manner as her husband can
with property belonging to him, but that she may make
contracts and incur liabilities, and the same may be enforced against her, the same as if she were a *feme sole.*
There is now no residuum of civil disability resting upon
her which is not recognized as existing against the husband.
The current runs steadily and strongly in the direction of
the emancipation of the wife, and the policy, as disclosed
by all recent legislation upon the subject in this State, is
to place her upon the same footing as if she were a *feme
sole*, not only with respect to her separate property, but as
it affects her right to make binding contracts; and the most
natural corollary to the situation is that the remedies for
the enforcement of liabilities incurred are made co-extensive
and co-equal with such enlarged conditions."

It thus appears that, putting to one side the elective
franchise, in the matter of personal and contractual rights
they stand on the same plane as the other sex. Their rights
in these respects can no more be infringed than the equal
rights of their brothers. We held in *Lochner* v. *New York*,
198 U. S. 45, that a law providing that no laborer shall be
required or permitted to work in bakeries more than sixty
hours in a week or ten hours in a day was not as to men a
legitimate exercise of the police power of the State, but an
unreasonable, unnecessary, and arbitrary interference with
the right and liberty of the individual to contract in relation to his labor, and as such was in conflict with, and void

under, the Federal Constitution. That decision is invoked by plaintiff in error as decisive of the question before us. But this assumes that the difference between the sexes does not justify a different rule respecting a restriction of the hours of labor.

In patent cases counsel are apt to open the argument with a discussion of the state of the art. It may not be amiss, in the present case, before examining the constitutional question, to notice the course of legislation as well as expressions of opinion from other than judicial sources. In the brief filed by Mr. Louis D. Brandeis, for the defendant in error, is a very copious collection of all these matters, an epitome of which is found in the margin.*

While there have been but few decisions bearing directly

* The following legislation of the States impose restriction in some form or another upon the hours of labor that may be required of women: Massachusetts, 1874, Rev. Laws 1902, chap. 106, sec. 24; Rhode Island, 1885, Acts and Resolves 1902, chap. 994, p. 73; Louisiana, 1886, Rev. Laws 1904, vol. i, sec. 4, p. 989; Connecticut, 1887, Gen. Stat. revision 1902, sec. 4691; Maine, 1887, Rev. Stat. 1903, chap. 40, sec. 48; New Hampshire, 1887, Laws 1907, chap. 94, p. 95; Maryland, 1888, Pub. Gen. Laws 1903, art. 100, sec. 1; Virginia, 1890, Code 1904, tit. 51 a, chap. 178 a, sec. 3657 b; Pennsylvania, 1897, Laws 1905, No. 226, p. 352; New York, 1899, Laws 1907, chap. 507, sec. 77, subdiv. 3, p. 1078; Nebraska, 1899, Comp. Stat. 1905, sec. 7955, p. 1986; Washington, Stat. 1901, chap. 68, sec. 1, p. 118; Colorado, Acts 1903, chap. 138, sec. 3, p. 310; New Jersey, 1892, Gen. Stat. 1895, p. 2350, secs. 66 and 67; Oklahoma, 1890, Rev. Stat. 1903, chap. 25, art. 58, sec. 729; North Dakota, 1877, Rev. Code 1905, sec. 9440; South Dakota, 1877, Rev. Code (Penal Code, sec. 764), p. 1185; Wisconsin, 1867, Code 1898, sec. 1728; South Carolina, Acts 1907, No. 233.

In foreign legislation Mr. Brandeis calls attention to these statutes: Great Britain, 1844, Law 1901, 1 Edw. VII, chap. 22; France, 1848, Act Nov. 2, 1892, and March 30, 1900; Switzerland, Canton of Glarus, 1848, Federal Law 1877, art. 2, sec. 1; Austria, 1855, Acts 1897, art. 96 a, secs. 1 to 3; Holland, 1889, art. 5, sec. 1; Italy, June 19, 1902, art. 7; Germany, Laws 1891.

Then follow extracts from over ninety reports of committees, bureaus of statistics, commissioners of hygiene, inspectors of factories, both in this country and in Europe, to the effect that long hours of labor are dangerous for women, primarily because of their special physical organization. The matter is discussed in these reports in different aspects, but all agree as to the danger. It would of course take too much space to give these reports in detail. Following them are extracts from similar reports discussing the general benefits of short hours from an economic aspect of the question. In many of these reports individual instances are given tending to support the general conclusion. Perhaps the general scope and character of all these reports may be summed up in what an inspector for Hanover says: "The reasons for the reduction of the working day to ten hours — (a) the physical organization of woman, (b) her maternal functions, (c) the rearing and education of the children, (d) the maintenance of the home — are all so important and so far-reaching that the need for such reduction need hardly be discussed."

upon the question, the following sustain the constitutionality of such legislation: *Commonwealth* v. *Hamilton Mfg. Co.*, 125 Mass. 383; *Wenham* v. *State*, 65 Neb. 394, 400, 406; *State* v. *Buchanan*, 29 Wash. 602; *Commonwealth* v. *Beatty*, 15 Pa. Sup. Ct. 5, 17; against them in the case of *Ritchie* v. *People*, 155 Ill. 98.

The legislation and opinions referred to in the margin may not be, technically speaking, authorities, and in them is little or no discussion of the constitutional question presented to us for determination, yet they are significant of a widespread belief that woman's physical structure, and the functions she performs in consequence thereof, justify special legislation restricting or qualifying the conditions under which she should be permitted to toil. Constitutional questions, it is true, are not settled by even a consensus of present public opinion, for it is the peculiar value of a written constitution that it places in unchanging form limitations upon legislative action, and thus gives a permanence and stability to popular government which otherwise would be lacking. At the same time, when a question of fact is debated and debatable, and the extent to which a special constitutional limitation goes is affected by the truth in respect to that fact, a widespread and long continued belief concerning it is worthy of consideration. We take judicial cognizance of all matters of general knowledge.

It is undoubtedly true, as more than once declared by this court, that the general right to contract in relation to one's business is part of the liberty of the individual, protected by the Fourteenth Amendment to the Federal Constitution; yet it is equally well settled that this liberty is not absolute and extending to all contracts, and that a State may, without conflicting with the provisions of the Fourteenth Amendment, restrict in many respects the individual's power of contract. Without stopping to discuss at length the extent to which a State may act in this respect, we refer to the following cases in which the question has been considered: *Allgeyer* v. *Louisiana,* 165 U. S. 578; *Holden* v. *Hardy,* 169 U. S. 366; *Lochner* v. *New York, supra.*

That woman's physical structure and the performance of maternal functions place her at a disadvantage in the struggle for subsistence is obvious. This is especially true when the burdens of motherhood are upon her. Even when they are not, by abundant testimony of the medical fraternity continuance for a long time on her feet at work, repeating this from day to day, tends to injurious effects upon the body, and as healthy mothers are essential to vigorous offspring, the physical well-being of woman becomes an object of public interest and care in order to preserve the strength and vigor of the race.

Still again, history discloses the fact that woman has always been dependent upon man. He established his control at the outset by superior physical strength, and this control in various forms, with diminishing intensity, has continued to the present. As minors, though not to the same extent, she has been looked upon in the courts as needing especial care that her rights may be preserved. Education was long denied her, and while now the doors of the school-room are opened and her opportunities for acquiring knowledge are great, yet even with that and the consequent increase of capacity for business affairs it is still true that in the struggle for subsistence she is not an equal competitor with her brother. Though limitations upon personal and contractual rights may be removed by legislation, there is that in her disposition and habits of life which will operate against a full assertion of those rights. She will still be where some legislation to protect her seems necessary to secure a real equality of right. Doubtless there are individual exceptions, and there are many respects in which she has an advantage over him; but looking at it from the viewpoint of the effort to maintain an independent position in life, she is not upon an equality. Differentiated by these matters from the other sex, she is properly placed in a class by herself, and legislation designed for her protection may be sustained, even when like legislation is not necessary for men and could not be sustained. It is impossible to close one's eyes to the fact that she still looks to her brother and depends upon him. Even though all restrictions on political, personal, and contractual rights were taken away, and she stood, so far as statutes are concerned, upon an absolutely equal plane with him, it would still be true that she is so constituted that she will rest upon and look to him for protection; that her physical structure and a proper discharge of her maternal functions — having in view not merely her own health, but the well-being of the race — justify legislation to protect her from the greed as well as the passion of man. The limitations which this statute places upon her contractual powers, upon her right to agree with her employer as to the time she shall labor, are not imposed solely for her benefit, but also largely for the benefit of all. Many words cannot make this plainer. The two sexes differ in structure of body, in the functions to be performed by each, in the amount of physical strength, in the capacity for long-continued labor, particularly when done standing, the influence of vigorous health upon the future well-being of the race, the self-reliance which enables one to assert full rights, and in the capacity to maintain the struggle for subsistence. This difference justifies a difference in legislation and upholds that which is designed to compensate for some of the burdens which rest upon her.

We have not referred in this discussion to the denial of the elective franchise in the State of Oregon, for while that may disclose a lack of political equality in all things with her brother, that is not of itself decisive. The reason runs deeper, and rests in the inherent difference between the two sexes, and in the different functions in life which they perform.

For these reasons, and without questioning in any respect the decision in *Lochner* v. *New York*, we are of the opinion that it cannot be adjudged that the act in question is in conflict with the Federal Constitution, so far as it respects the work of a female in a laundry, and the judgment of the Supreme Court of Oregon is

Affirmed.

True Copy.

Test:

JAMES H. McKENNEY,

CLERK, SUPREME COURT, U. S.